Who Benefits from the Sanitized Language of Violence?

International Studies on Military Ethics

THE SERIES IS EDITED UNDER THE AUSPICES OF THE INTERNATIONAL SOCIETY FOR MILITARY ETHICS IN EUROPE (EUROISME)

VOLUME 14

EURO ISME
International Society for Military Ethics in Europe

The titles published in this series are listed at *brill.com/isme*

Who Benefits from the Sanitized Language of Violence?

By

Matthew Fyjis-Walker

BRILL | NIJHOFF

LEIDEN | BOSTON

The views expressed in this paper are those of the author and do not necessarily represent those of the UK Ministry of Defence or any other department of Her Britannic Majesty's Government of the United Kingdom. Furthermore such views should not be considered as constituting an official endorsement of factual accuracy, opinion, conclusion or recommendation of the UK Ministry of Defence or any other department of Her Britannic Majesty's Government of the United Kingdom.

Library of Congress Cataloging-in-Publication Data

Names: Fyjis-Walker, Matthew, author.
Title: Who benefits from the sanitized language of violence? / Matthew Fyjis-Walker.
Description: Leiden ; Boston : Brill/Nijhoff, 2024. | Series: International studies on military ethics, 2214-7926 ; volume 14 | Includes bibliographical references.
Identifiers: LCCN 2024020943 (print) | LCCN 2024020944 (ebook) | ISBN 9789004696419 (hardback) | ISBN 9789004696426 (ebook)
Subjects: LCSH: Military law–Great Britain. | Military ethics–Great Britain. | Law–Great Britain–Language. | Civil-military relations–Great Britain. | Great Britain–Military policy. | War (International law) | Violence (Law) | Euphemism.
Classification: LCC KD6000 .F95 2024 (print) | LCC KD6000 (ebook) | DDC 355.001/4–dc23/eng/20240512
LC record available at https://lccn.loc.gov/2024020943
LC ebook record available at https://lccn.loc.gov/2024020944

Typeface for the Latin, Greek, and Cyrillic scripts: "Brill". See and download: brill.com/brill-typeface.

ISSN 2214-7926
ISBN 978-90-04-69641-9 (hardback)
ISBN 978-90-04-69642-6 (e-book)
DOI 10.1163/9789004696426

This book is printed on acid-free paper and produced in a sustainable manner.

This thesis has been awarded the first prize of the year 2022 in EuroISME's annual contest for the best student's thesis (MA). For information about the contest, please visit www.euroisme.eu

The jury of EuroISME's annual prize for the best student's thesis on military ethics consists of

1. Colonel Rev. Prof. Dr. P.J. McCormack, MBE, (chairman, United Kingdom)
2. Brigadier General (ret.) Benoît Royal (France)
3. Senior Chaplain Lt.Col. Dr. Janne Aalto (Finland)
4. Dr. Veronika Bock (Germany)
5. Mil Superior MMag. Stefan Gugerel (Austria)
6. Dr. Asta Maskaliūnaitė (Estonia)
7. Maj.Gen. (res) Dr. Juan Moliner Gonzalez (Spain)
8. Ms. Ivana Gošić (Serbia, secretary)

Enquiries: secretariat.ethicsprize@euroisme.eu
www.euroisme.eu

The prize is supported by

Contents

Introduction

> The limits of my language are the limits of my world.
>
> WITTGENSTEIN[1]

∴

If the electorate's language and vocabulary of war is limited, how can they understand the expanse of violence conducted in their name? Language central to the relationship between the government and the electorate. This relationship, through the lens of language, has not been thoroughly examined as regards the use of violence.[2] This paper explores the role of a particularly limiting vocabulary on the electorate's understanding of war, sanitised language.

Sanitised language is not a well-defined class of vocabulary but is made up of language that seeks to clean up the appearance of events. Sanitised language's tools include abstract terms, euphemisms that stretch social norms, the dulling of emotional content, and obscuration of difficult issues. Born of the researcher's acknowledgement of his own poor explanation of conflict, the study is not alone in identifying a problem with the military's language. Matthew Parris summed up what many lament, when he spoke of briefings by the military in Afghanistan, "It is easy to be blinded by … the acronyms and euphemisms … [the language] tells of baffled expatriates … in flight from reality."[3]

This paper first examines the government-electorate relationship through the lens of the Armed Forces Covenant, which is a facsimile of Clausewitz's secondary trinity (people-government-military). It argues that the written word does not reflect the practice; the relationship is frayed. Krieg and Rickli overstate the fraying of the bond in their concept of surrogacy, but in-so-doing provide a contrasting concept that, when "added" to Clausewitz, offers nuance and reflects reality of the relationship more accurately. Surrogacy's tools are drones and proxy forces; the paper concludes that language has similar properties, it can reduce the obvious costs of war to the public authorities.

1 C. Coker. *War in an age of risk,* (Polity Press: Cambridge. 2009): 6.

2 Heuser, *Reading Clausewitz*: 53.

3 M. Parris "In the fog remember; victory is impossible in Afghanistan," *The Times*, 4 July 2009.

The paper builds on existing arguments to fill a gap in the literature. Key themes outlined in Chapter 2 are: sanitised language, language war and power, political myth, public opinion the media and the influence of trust and transparency. There are two major methodological gaps – the lack of a representative sample of UK public opinion specific to this question, and the small size of the sample that was taken – these mean that the study uses proxies to make its arguments, and that conclusions must be tentative.

Chapter 4 focuses on the public authorities' language about the 2011 Libya and Counter-Daesh campaigns, from which two trends emerge. First, language *justifying* violence is typically clear and follows the ingroup-outgroup formulation (us-them). Second, language *explaining* the state's use of violence is often less clear. Chapter 5 explores factors that contribute to these apparent trends, particularly the social and political influences on the public authorities. The paper then turns to the impacts of using sanitised language, Michaels makes a compelling argument that language constrains thinking in the military,[4] and Orwell argues that language reflects thinking.[5] This paper considers different issues, that while sanitised language can be useful, the paper argues that its use leads to a democratic deficit and reduces public authorities' freedoms. And possibly unnecessarily so, as it appears the public can tolerate considerable costs, if arguments are clear.

It would be naïve to think answers are simple. Further work is needed to draw concrete conclusions, but it is hoped that this challenge to the status quo leads to a more effective defence of the value, and therefore acceptance, of hard power, the threat or use of violence as an instrument of the state. If the public are inoculated to the value of violence and the quality of democracy is undermined, advantage is ceded the UK's adversaries. The paper is written in the spirit of productive iconoclasm not revolution.

---

4 J. Michaels, *The Discourse Trap* (Palgrave MacMillan: London. 2013).

5 G. Orwell, *Politics and the English language* (Penguin: London. 2013).

CHAPTER 1

Does the Model of Surrogacy Offer Value to the Analysis of Civil-Military Relations in the UK?

> Clausewitz's secondary trinity ... could usefully be developed much further, to explain and analyse civil-military relations.
>
> B. HEUSER[1]

Clausewitz provides a traditional lens through which to analyse civil-military relations, but challengers claim his mode of analysis is outdated and requires anything from minor adaptation to consigning to the rubbish tip.[2] Anders Krieg and Jean-Marc Rickli offer one such challenge through the idea of surrogacy, potentially offering further insights into civil-military relations. This first chapter explores the nature of the civil-military relations in the United Kingdom (UK), which provides the framework for the rest of the paper's examination of the language of violence.

The UK has enshrined in law the principles contained in one of Clausewitz's most famous constructs, commonly known as the secondary trinity. The UK Government did this by creating the Armed Forces Covenant, committing itself to a set of relationships and obligations in the form that Clausewitz described, recognising Clausewitz's value today. While the UK Government has chosen one approach, there are others, and different aspects of the relations have been widely studied. Mao, for example, was intrigued by the relationship between the people and the military, and there is the whole field of civil-military relations, but the relationship between the government and the electorate, with regard to the use of force, has had less thorough examination.[3]

This chapter explores Clausewitz's secondary trinity, in the context of the primary, grappling with its critics, arguing that it remains a valuable, if strained,

1 B. Heuser, *Reading Clausewitz* (London: Pimlico. 2002): 56.

2 H. Strachan, *Making strategy work: civil-military relations in Britain and the United States* (Cambridge: Cambridge University Press. 2013): 46.

3 Heuser, *Reading Clausewitz*, 53.

mode of analysis, despite dissent from notable academics. It agrees with Strachan, Bassford and Villacres that Clausewitz did not intend his key text *Vom Kriege* ('On War') to be a piece of doctrine, but rather a tool of analysis; its approach is dialectical not hierarchical, and as such is theoretically valuable.[4] The paper goes on to examine the strength and nature of nation-government relationship in the UK through a Clausewitzian lens, exposing some gaps between the structures and the reality. Krieg and Rickli's model of surrogacy is then used as an alternate lens to discuss whether the UK Government might be straying away from ideas associated with the secondary trinity to deal with the modern political challenges of using force. In so doing the paper argues that the UK has moved away from a strict facsimile of the Clausewitzian trinity towards one that increasingly operates with a weaker connection between elements of the secondary trinity than was imagined by Clausewitz.

1 Clausewitz's Trinities Explored

Clausewitz declares that war should be:

> regarded as a whole and in relation to the tendencies that dominate within it, a fascinating trinity – composed of (1) primordial violence, hatred and enmity (2) … the play of chance and probability … (3) its element of subordination as an instrument of policy, which makes it subject to pure reason.[5]

To these tendencies a series of human agents are associated, in what can be thought of as a secondary trinity. *Primordial violence* is the emotional driver for conflict and is most commonly associated with the people of a nation, whose beliefs influence a state to fight. The *play of chance and probability*, an expression of the challenges faced by those doing the fighting, is most commonly associated with the military, for whom war is full of friction. In *Rebooting Clausewitz* Coker says "friction … is the only conception which in a general way corresponds to that which distinguishes real war from war on paper."[6] Friction

4 H. Strachan, Sir Michael Howard lectures 18 November 2020 and C. Bassford and E. Villacres, "Reclaiming the Clausewitzian Trinity" in: *Parameters*, Autumn (1995): 17.

5 C. Bassford, 'The primacy of Policy and the Trinity' in: "Clausewitz's mature thought," in: Strachan, H., Herberg-Rothe, A., *Clausewitz in the Twenty-First Century* (Oxford: Oxford University Press, 2007): 78.

6 C. Coker, *Rebooting Clausewitz: "On War" in the twenty-first century* (New York: Oxford University Press. 2017): 128.

is made up of the unpredictable issues that throw a plan off its intended course, it makes the practise of war difficult. *Its subordination* to reason is typically connected to government, who determine policy.[7]

The nation-government relationship is important in war; in democratic societies the electorate is expected to play a role, at very least by extension, in rational decision making and in the accountability of government in war; Lord Chilcot's Iraq Inquiry Report was clear on this, "in a democratic system, public support and understanding for a major military operation are essential".[8] Clausewitz argues that policy and strategy cannot be the preserve of the Government and its associated professional elites; in creating policy and strategy, the Government develops a professional conversation with its military and a separate, no less important, conversation with the electorate to whom government is ultimately accountable.[9] This conversation is explored in greater detail in later chapters. Extrapolating from Clausewitz's proposition that the people of a nation fight well if they know what they are fighting for, one can determine that professional militaries should need the support, rather than manpower, of the nation to succeed.[10] A nation that understands why its military uses violence is more likely to support them; this again gets more attention later in the paper. These ideas have been used to explain military success and defeat; Colonel Harry Summers' contested analysis of the Vietnam War concluded that an apparent overlooking of the trinity was a key factor in American failure. Specifically, he argues that the lack of identification of the public with the war's aims meant that public support for the war, and therefore ultimately the war itself, was difficult to sustain; this was the Administration's undoing. General David Petraeus uses the same Clausewitzian lens for analysis but arrives at a different answer suggesting that the breakdown in the link between the military and the Government was the most significant factor.[11] These positions are in some ways not mutually exclusive and show the value of the trinities as lenses for understanding war, war-making, and associated relationships.

7 Bassford and Villacres, "Reclaiming the Clausewitzian Trinity": 10. T. Mahnken, "Strategic Theory" in: Baylis, J., Cohen, E., Gray, C., Witz (eds.), *Strategy in the contemporary world*, 2nd ed. (Oxford: Oxford University Press. 2007): 72.

8 Bassford and Villacres, "Reclaiming the Clausewitzian Trinity,": 13; J. Chilcot, *The Report of the Iraq Inquiry* (UK: House of Commons. 2016): 129.

9 R. Harris and H. Strachan, *The Utility of Military Force and Public Understanding in Todays Britain* (RAND Europe. 2020): ii and 16.

10 *Ibid.,* ii and 17.

11 Heuser, *Reading Clausewitz*: 54.

In contrast to this, others argue, particularly in a modern context, that Clausewitz should be treated with caution. Two criticisms, among others, are laid at Clausewitz's door regarding the people, or nation/electorate, in his writings. First, van Creveld argues that Clausewitz fails to reflect on the role of the people in war in sufficient depth, "The third element in Clausewitzian trinitarian war, namely the people, did not come into the equation at all".[12] Van Creveld specifically set out that peoples' roles as victims are overlooked, though this may be because Clausewitz was heavily influenced by his own context, Napoleonic era war generally did not affect civilians in this way. But Raymond Aron counters that while Clausewitz does not explore the impact of violence on the public, if they are not directly involved, the analysis is implicit in his writing.[13] And Coker notes Clausewitz is interested in civilians.[14] Second, Keegan and van Creveld challenge Clausewitz's notion that government, public and military are always distinct, and going further, whether in certain circumstances they exist at all. This is seen as a shortfall in Clausewitz's analysis, particularly when studying wars of the people, where the boundaries between these groups are harder to determine or indeed may not exist,[15] as van Creveld says "the most characteristic fact … is precisely that these distinctions did not exist".[16] Aron acknowledges here that Clausewitz's analysis is not fulsome but this criticism tends to focus on Clausewitz as doctrine rather than dialectic, and misses that almost any conflict that is organised within a society will have a leadership of some form, a series of fighters (or those that execute operations), and a support base.[17] Bassford and Villacres strongly argue that these looser descriptions are worthy synonyms for Clausewitz's original terms, and that therefore the analytical lens remains relevant.[18] This only makes sense if the analyst appreciates the difference between the two trinities.

12 M. van Creveld, *Transformation of War* (New York Free Press. 1991): 63.
13 Heuser, *Reading Clausewitz*: 53.
14 Coker, *Rebooting Clausewitz:* 119.
15 *Ibid.*, 53.
16 Van Creveld, "The Transformation of War Revisited," in: *Small Wars & Insurgencies* 13, no. 2 (2002): 8.
17 Heuser, *Reading Clausewitz*: 53.
18 Bassford and Villacres, 'Reclaiming the Clausewitzian Trinity': 15 and 17.

2 Nation-Government Relations in UK, Clausewitzian?

Turning now to the specifics of the UK, the secondary trinity provides the UK Government with inspiration for the Armed Forces Covenant, a codification of civil-military relations in a facsimile of Clausewitz's secondary trinity and is thus a valuable mechanism to visualise and test the value of Clausewitz to understand civil-military relations in the UK. The Armed Forces Covenant sets out the obligations the Nation (here taken to represent the electorate), the Armed Forces Community and the Government have to each other (at Figure 1); its key principles are enshrined in law through the Armed Forces Act 2011.[19] While the Covenant's primary aim is to support the Armed Forces Community, the paper necessarily focuses on the relationship between the Nation and its Government.[20] The Nation is to *sustain* (the Government) and *understand* (the Government's) policies, while the Government commits to *justify* and *explain* (its actions to the Nation), and *lead* (the nation). The Covenant makes clear that no obligation is contingent on another, but, as the author, it is particularly beholden on the Government to uphold its commitments.[21]

Despite being social-contractian in nature, where the Government holds the monopoly on violence and the public holds it to account, the Covenant makes no mention of how the Nation should exercise its democratic responsibilities, or indeed how the Nation should be engaged vis-a-vis the use of violence or making/waging of war.[22] So, while it espouses a Clausewitzian doctrine, the UK Government does not clarify the mechanisms through which this critical relationship between Nation and Government should operate, leaving room for the Government to manoeuvre the terms of the relationship. In this context, Harris and Strachan argue that there are three ways in which the electorate and Government are connected to one another in the UK, in terms of the use of violence. First, the Nation has a role in holding to account the Government, second through communication with the Government about the use of violence, and third because the Nation bears the costs of violence.[23] The extent to which these bind the public to the Government is fluid, the

19 United Kingdom, Ministry of Defence, *The Armed Forces Covenant* (2000): 10.

20 Dr Sarah Ingham, interview with the author, April 27 2021.

21 *Ibid.*

22 V. Rauta, "Delegation in distress; an ever-growing semantic field?" in: Rauta, A. *et al.* "A Symposium-debating 'surrogate warfare' and the transformation of war" in: *Defence Studies.* 19, no4 (2019): 417.

23 Harris and Strachan, "The Utility of Military Force and Public Understanding in Today's Britain," <https://www.rand.org/content/dam/rand/pubs/research_reports/RRA200/RRA213-1/RAND_RRA213-1.pdf> pp. 19–22.

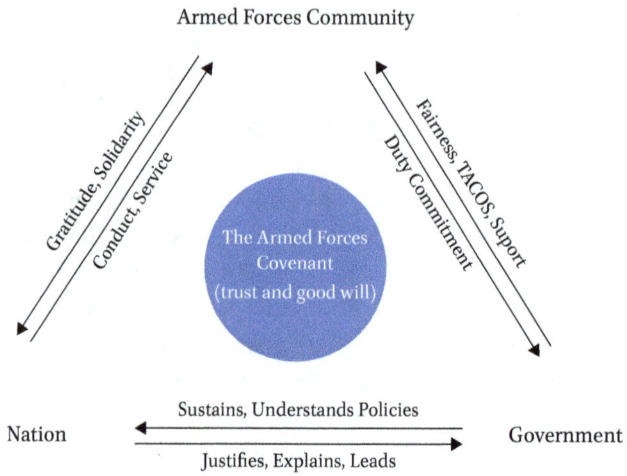

FIGURE 1 The Armed Forces Covenant diagram and obligations

evidence that follows undermines arguments that a strong relationship exists, but falls short of dismissing it.

First, the United Kingdom is a representative, not a participative democracy, giving the Government flexibility in how to enable, or otherwise, public oversight of Governmental affairs, how it must justify itself, and also affecting how engaged the public appear to be, or are, with matters of violence.[24] In general, the Nation elects Members of Parliament who should hold the government to account on their behalf,[25] but Parliamentary oversight of the use of force has changed with the advent of more direct communications channels, a general aversion to matters of violence, and a lack of Members of Parliament who have military experience with which to examine the Government's use of force.[26] Routine parliamentary oversight of the use of force is considered to be relatively weak, the 2013 vote on action in Syria was a substantial departure from the norm. Select Committees do provide this function to some extent, but only on an episodic basis, and Ministers can side step Committees;[27] Stewart argues that public accountability cannot rely on Parliament.[28] Indeed, the All-Party

24 *Ibid.*, 21.

25 A. Forster, *Armed Forces and Society in Europe*. (Basingstoke: Palgrave Macmillan. 2006): 26.

26 Harris and Strachan, *The Utility of Military Force and Public Understanding in Today's Britain*: 20.

27 *Ibid.*, 21.

28 R. Stewart, interview with author 27 May 2021.

Parliamentary Group on Drones accuses the government of poor transparency on these matters and particularly in Committees.[29] As a consequence, the Nation has limited formal democratic means to interrogate the Government, and Government escapes having to thoroughly justify its actions, as it commits to in the Covenant.

The second issue is that of communication between nation and Government, where substantial change in recent years has strained the traditional view of the relationship. A proliferation of technologies and channels offers individual members of the electorate the opportunity to access directly the Government to try to understand and challenge elite decision making and use of violence, as is their commitment in the Covenant. Government and its officials also use these channels, but are much more circumspect, perhaps seeking avoiding the need to justify. Government sees as much risk as reward in channels; elites have lost the ability to control narratives and debates as tightly as before, indeed some argue that this unsettles their dominance in the Nation-Government relationship. The traditional press still plays an important role in mediating between the elite and the public but they too are disenfranchised by modern technologies and their use by the electorate. In the UK, Government and Nation are adjusting to these new technologies, and how to use them in communicating over the use of force. While the Nation has the opportunity to exercise its commitments in the Covenant, to understand policies, and can be assertive in new ways, the Government appears to be cautious of engaging, leaving many unsatisfied with the nature of this interaction.[30] The role of the press is discussed further in Chapter 2.

Third, the nation bears the costs of violence, principal among these are the deaths sustained in, and the material costs of, war. Deaths of UK service-persons became highly political during the most violent periods of recent wars in Afghanistan and Iraq, as David Whetham explains in Neither Victors nor Victims. Whetham outlines that the electorate was highly engaged with the Government over these 'home-team' deaths; such was their concern that the costs were too great to bear that the Ministry of Defence appeared to try to reduce the public visibility of the deaths by quietly changing the route that dead service persons took to the Coroner on arrival in the UK.[31] Turning to

29 All Party Parliamentary Group on Drones (APPG), *The UK's Use of Armed Drones: working with partners*, <www.appgdrones.org.uk> (2018): 8.

30 Harris and Strachan, *The Utility of Military Force and Public Understanding in Today's Britain*: 21–22.

31 D. Whetham, "Neither Victors nor Victims," in: A. Hom, C. O'Driscoll and K. Mills, *Moral Victories: The Ethics of Winning Wars* (2017): 176–198.

material costs, recently the nation has rarely borne obvious financial costs of war, Chancellors rarely explain taxation or fiscal policy with mention to war, this was certainly the case for the Afghanistan and Iraq wars whose costs were absorbed by the Treasury without fanfare.[32] The 2020 Spending Review was one of the more politically charged and publicly relevant financial battles between the Treasury and the Ministry of Defence, where despite the COVID pandemic, Defence received an increase in funding over a 10-year investment programme.[33] Public, not press, reaction appeared muted, perhaps which is consistent with analysis of the UK electorate's pre-election key issues, where only five percent of people registered Defence as important, languishing towards the bottom of a YouGov poll.[34] The consequence is that the public only considers the costs of war when they become real to them, personal tragedy drives public sentiment, and the Government does little to highlight these, perhaps even actively trying to avoid such issues, and as a result not actively engaging in the relationship. The paper picks up on this issue later when it examines how the main issues and arguments come together to form a conclusion.

3 Surrogacy an Alternate Model?

This interpretation of the evidence suggests that a set of democratic structures that provide a framework, within which Clausewitzian Nation-Government relations can flourish, exists, but that evidence for the actual, rather than potential structure of the relationship between UK Government and electorate is weak. Indeed, the Government does not appear to be attempting to strengthen it. Other analytical lenses suggest that the Government is in fact not pursuing a relationship in the pure Clausewitzian form, but rather that there is a deliberate effort to change it by the Government. Martin Shaw's *Western Way of War* is one such lens, though he acknowledges Clausewitz's value and is heavily focussed on technological aspects of war,[35] another, proposed by Andreas Krieg and Jean-Marc Rickli, argues that governments are employing

32 Harris, and Strachan, *The Utility of Military Force and Public Understanding in Today's Britain*: 21.

33 United Kingdom, HM Government Press release. "PM to announce largest military investment in 30 years (2020)," <www.gov.uk>.

34 YouGov, *Which issues will decide the general election?* November 7, 2019 <www.yougov.co.uk>.

35 Coker, *Rebooting Clausewitz:* xi.

non-trinitarian concepts of war to cope with manifold modern challenges, specifically by re-shaping the relationships between the actors associated with organised violence.

Krieg and Rickli's argue that their concept of "Surrogate Warfare" is a "break from the classical [Clausewitzian] trinitarian model of war". They define surrogate warfare as "the Conceptual umbrella for all forces of externalisation of the burden of warfare to supplementary as well as substitutionary forces and platforms",[36] these include technologies such as drones, and proxy forces in military vernacular. In essence, surrogacy is an effort by Government to reduce the costs of war for itself, the electorate and military. Efforts to reduce the costs of war are both rational and ancient, but Krieg and Rickli argue that these efforts have become the norm in, rather than peripheral to, the use of violence, allowing the Government to remain the primary security actor without associated trinitarian costs. Increasingly these costs are political, as well as financial and human; the combination of costs makes externalising the burden to a surrogate politically attractive, as the surrogate sits outside a strict interpretation of the trinity. By "externalising the burden of warfare" Krieg and Rickli suggest that Governments move political and emotional pressures exerted by the electorate onto government to surrogates, thus changing the relationship from electorate-government to electorate-surrogate: "Surrogate warfare cuts the socio-political ties [of the Clausewitzian trinity]". They argue that an example of this is the transfer of local and global public opinion from a sponsor-government to surrogate, as can be seen the case of Kurdish surrogates fighting ISIS in Iraq and Syria, sponsored by the UK (and USA) who follow a "no boots on the ground" policy in Syria and Iraq.[37] There is clear evidence that the UK is also developing a wider range of technological surrogates, in part to reduce the likelihood of deaths of service persons during conflict, these include upgrading the "Reaper" drone fleet, developing an unmanned "wingman" for future combat aircraft, and remote underwater vehicles.[38] Surrogacy appears to be a central part of the UK's future, and current, method of warfare.

This proposed deviation from Clausewitz is unsurprisingly contested. Vladimir Rauta is not taken with the idea that surrogacy offers a new break away from the trinity, though is content that, in the modern context, it represents "*neo-trinitarianism*". Rauta's challenges the looseness of the definition of surrogacy, which rides roughshod over recent efforts (by Heuser among

36 A. Krieg, and J-M. Rickli, "Surrogate warfare: the art of war in the 21 Century?" in: *Defence Studies*. 18, no2. (2018): 115.

37 *Ibid.*, 116 and 117.

38 APPG, *The UK's Use of Armed Drones: working with partners*: 22.

others) to delineate between types of surrogate, and misses that surrogates might be the dominant agents in a relationship, garnering external support to meet their own needs.[39] Christopher Rickland notes that the concept can barely be considered new, is vulnerable to the same criticisms levelled at the "new wars scholars", and while it has some merit, adds to the "conceptual turmoil in the field" rather than clarifying it.[40] Krieg and Rickli offer a useful analytical counterpoint to the Clausewitzian trinitarian lens, but their arguments are insufficient to consign Clausewitz's insights to history.

4 Or a Synthesis of the Two?

It appears from this analysis that Clausewitz's trinity and Krieg and Rickli's "surrogacy" can co-exist to some extent: both models are useful tools in understanding the relationship between electorate and government in the UK. Surrogacy, if less stringently interpreted, could provide an adjunct to Clausewitz in understanding how the UK Government and electorates manage their relations with each other. Evidence from the UK demonstrates that the structure of the democratic system of government provides a framework upon which a fluid relationship between the Government and the nation can hang. The Government and nation are active in determining the strength of this relationship, consistent with others, the UK electorate appears to be currently somewhat apathetic[41] and the Government seeks to reduce pressure on itself (exercised by the electorate) by the use of surrogates. But the Government, as in the Armed Forces Covenant, realises it cannot be totally disconnected from the electorate, and is wary of completely disenfranchising the electorate, as Summers argues US Administrations did at great cost during the Vietnam War. This is as much a democratic as it is a Clausewitzian concern. Thus, the UK Government seeks to be able to control the strength and focus of its relationship with the electorate to its advantage, acknowledging the importance of that relationship, but also exploiting the advantages of surrogacy. Perhaps this better represents a diluting, rather than complete externalisation of the relationship.

---

39 V. Rauta, "Delegation in distress: an ever-growing semantic field": 418.

40 C. Rickland, "Iran's surrogate warfare and the future of the concept" in: Rauta, A. *et al.* "A Symposium – debating 'surrogate warfare' and the transformation of war" in: *Defence Studies.* 19, no 4 (2019): 420/421.

41 J. Mueller, *War, Presidents and Public Opinion*, New York: John Wiley (1973): 59 and YouGov "which-issues-will-decide general-election".

This chapter has argued that despite serious fraying at the edges there remains a democratic structure in which a Clausewitzian framework for a relationship between Government and Nation exists. Despite vociferous challenge by modern scholars such as Keegan and van Creveld, Clausewitz remains defensible as an analytical tool, a dialectic not hierarchical method, for understanding the use of violence. Harris and Strachan provide evidence for a strained Clausewitzian relationship between the Government and the electorate in the UK, but a relationship none the less. A weak but functioning parliamentary oversight system, a cautious use of public communication and low-key explanations of the financial costs of the use of violence demonstrate that the Government is aware of its obligations to the electorate but appears to do little to deepen the relationship. Krieg and Rickli's alternative lens, "surrogacy", does offer further explanation for how the Government seeks to manage its relationship with the nation, by offloading the costs of violence onto technological and human surrogates. While these ideas are neither new nor unexpected, they argue that their dominance as a mode of violence elevates them to being a new lens for analysis, in competition to Clausewitz. Counter arguments focus on the lack of novelty, the unhelpful breadth of the concept and the idea that surrogates can be actors with their own agency. Despite these challenges, there is evidence of behaviour consistent with the use of surrogates by the UK. The UK routinely supports proxies and partners to do the UK's bidding, as in Iraq, and there appear to be increased efforts to develop technological surrogates within the future equipment fleets of the UK. But this neither leads to the conclusion that Clausewitz's trinity is an outmoded analysis, nor that Governments can ignore the electorate in formulating and executing strategies for the use of violence. A less strict interpretation of Krieg and Rickli's surrogacy model could sit well alongside a looser Clausewitzian analysis of relationships if both models accepted some compromise.

Accepting that neither is mutually exclusive, nor dogma, provides scope to analyse the Government-electorate relationship in the UK in this more nuanced fashion. This paper uses this adapted Clausewitzian framework to examine the role of language in binding or excluding the nation from its role in the use of violence, perhaps as a first step on a ladder of surrogacy. It turns now to a series of other concepts fundamental to the arguments the paper makes later.

CHAPTER 2

Literature Review

In his essay *The Gulf War did not take place,* Baudrillard claims that the public imagery of the Gulf war was so effectively sanitised by Allied governments that it did not reflect the actual conflict.[1] This study weaves this idea with other well-developed concepts, applying them as lenses to its specific subject, the use of sanitised language in the UK's official discourse on violence. Much of the literature focusses on America, while this is useful, it does not illuminate tendencies evident in the UK, as Kagan says, "On the all-important question of power … the efficacy of power, the morality of power, the desirability of power, American and European perspectives are diverging … the US is from Mars and the Europeans from Venus."[2] It is in the analysis of the specifics of modern UK issues, that the study offers synthesis and indicators of where research could be advanced. This chapter sets up later discussions by asking: what is said about the relationship between power and language? About euphemism, abstract and sanitising language? What is the influence of the modern context, specifically, political myths, public opinion, drones, media and move from existential and violent societies and war to instrumental and less violent? How important are the concepts of transparency and trust to this issue?

1 Language, War and Power

Michaels argues that to understand war, one has to understand the language of war. In a democracy, the public authorities should communicate to be understood.[3] Habermas draws a distinction between two types of language, communicative and strategic. He argues that public institutions are less and less orientated towards producing meaning (communicative language) but rather more orientated to achieving self-defined success (strategic language).[4] Foucault argues that discourse and language underpin institutional power relations. Laity argues that the purpose of political language is to persuade,[5]

1 J. Baudrillard, *The Gulf War did not take place* (Indiana University Press: Indiana. 1995).

2 A. Forster, *Armed Forces and Society in Europe* (Palgrave Macmillan: UK. 2005): 2.

3 J. Michaels, *The Discourse trap and the US military* (Palgrave Macmillan: UK. 2013): 1.

4 A. Mayr, *Language and Power: An Introduction to Institutional Discourse* (London: Continuum. 2008): 5.

5 M. Laity, interview with author 8 April 2021.

and can be a mechanism to achieve power over an audience. But this is not the only perspective, Giddens argues that institutions can emancipate as well as dominate through their use of language. So, language can both emancipate and dominate; this study locates the concept of domination with Habermas' strategic language, and emancipation with Habermas' communicative language.[6] Returning to the Armed Forces Covenant, the public might expect the Government to use strategic language to *justify* and communicative language to *explain,* but the study finds strategic language where it expected to find communicative.

Jackson argues that language of violence is never neutral, its binary nature means that the use of one term devalues another. Words are chosen to convey and hide meaning.[7] Laity argues that officials and representatives of public authorities should adapt their language to their audiences, where the motive is honest and information clear. But where the motive or clarity are lacking the communicator should be criticised.[8]

2 Sanitised Language

George Orwell bemoans and deconstructs poor use of English in *Politics and the English Language,* arguing that its abuse exposes incoherent thinking and disingenuity.[9] He highlights euphemism and abstraction as linguistic tools that dull the senses. They are two indicators of what this paper calls sanitised language, which is not a specific class of vocabulary but is consists of language that seeks to clean up the appearance of events. Redfern's short definition "euphemism provides a way of speaking about the unspeakable"[10] gives a sense of the value of euphemism but fails to address its controversial side, specifically that euphemism provides a means of not speaking clearly about the unspeakable. Abrantes suggests that euphemisms are words, or phrases, used to hide or reduce the impact of something unpleasant, generally through these tactics: speakers name unpleasant referents in more pleasant ways, focus

6 Mayr, *Language and power:* 6.

7 R. Jackson, *Writing the War on Terrorism: Language, politics and Counter-Terrorism* (Manchester University Press: Manchester. 2005): 2.

8 Laity, interview.

9 Orwell, *Politics and the English Language.*

10 A. Abrantes, "Euphemism and co-operation in discourse" in: Grillo (ed.) *Power without domination: dialogism and the empowering property of communication* (John Benjamins: Amsterdam: 2005): 85.

on its least unpleasant aspects, distract away from detail with generalisation or provide metaphor to avoid any specifics at all. She goes on to note that euphemism sits, uncomfortably at times, on the spectrum between truth and lie. Where the purpose, referent and meaning are socially transparent, euphemism is welcome. However, this is not always the case in institutional, or strategic, use of euphemism, which is a tool of de-humanisation of war, more of which in later chapters.[11]

Turning to abstraction, Neisser defines it as "representations that accomplish the near disappearance of particular facts except insofar as they take their place in a theory about how the particulars fit together in a larger whole". This captures how important detail is hidden within the noise.[12] Norris argues that those engaged in directing war seek to hide the true referent or meaning from the audience. She says that public authorities try to extinguish or blur the "real-making sign of warfare – namely the injured and dead body – into an unreality, unknowability and undecipherability".[13] The paper picks this up later.

Colley identifies techniques used to construct coherent narratives, they fall into two broad camps, those that serve to amplify the positive narrative communicators seek to establish, such as inclusion, linking, sharpening and clarifying. And those designed to reduce the impact of negative interpretations on the narrative, including omission, silencing and flattening. Audiences expect to see the former in the UK's efforts to *justify* activity, evidence for the latter is more problematic for a democratic discourse.[14] This paper exposes the use of these techniques later in Chapter 4.

3 Institutional Power

The techniques identified above are used by public authorities in seeking to control narratives and discourses of violence.[15] Mayr argues that language is a tool *with* which, and discourse is an environment *in* which, institutions and governments exercise power over their constituencies; institutional practices

11 *Ibid.*, 86.

12 P. Neisser, "Targets" in: J. Collins and R. Glover (eds.), *Collateral Language* (New York University Press: New York. 2002): 139.

13 M. Norris, "Military Censorship and the Body Count in the Persian Gulf War" in: *Cultural Critique*, Autumn, no. 19 (1991): 224.

14 T. Colley, "Is Britain a force for good? Investigating British citizens' narrative understanding of war," in: *Defence Studies* 17.1 (2017): 7–8.

15 K. Sengupta, interview with author, 10 May 2021.

and processes play a determining role in how events are understood. Through communication, institutions seek to legitimize their existence and practices, and also seek to transform or recontextualise social practices and meanings. This is done by reinforcing particular perspectives and by guarding, or protecting, others. Weber suggests that institutions in a democracy need public acceptance and therefore explicit or implicit legitimacy to wield power.[16] Jackson supports this position, arguing that state-led violence needs political and social consensus, language is the tool that achieves this.[17]

Van Djik says that dominant actors (Governments) "discursively construct and reproduce their own positions of dominance"; dominance and power allow elites to drive narratives, justifying and explaining what they choose to do.[18] Political myths are central to driving narratives, in part because the public latch onto ideas communicated as stories more than those transmitted as facts.[19] Within myth abstract language plays an important role in cementing the dominance of the elite narrators; sanitisation is a way of exerting power.[20]

4 Political Myth

Myth is an intuitive tool of reasoning, it provides significance (justification) to events, helping simplify the complex, but in so doing it over-simplifies, and often is rationally flawed.[21] The adept use of political myth is important in framing the electorate's understanding of the use of violence. The relationship between myth, meaning and events is widely discussed in the literature. Esch agrees with Jackson, arguing that events and facts cannot be thought to hold intrinsic meaning, facts never "speak for themselves".[22] Bottici and Challand state that myth has considerable unseen power in shaping discourse and reality.[23] Understanding is constructed, myths help determine understanding.[24]

16 Mayr, *Language and power*: 1–2.
17 Jackson, *Writing the War on Terrorism*: 2.
18 Mayr, *Language and power*: 3.
19 Laity, interview; T. Colley interview with author, 14 April 2021; J. Shea interview with author, 7 April 2021.
20 P. Neisser, "Targets": 138.
21 J. Esch, "Legitimising the "War on terror": political Myth in Official level Rhetoric" in: *Political Psychology* 31. 3 (2010): 360, 362.
22 *Ibid.*, 357.
23 C. Bottici and B. Challand, "Rethinking Political Myth: The Clash of Civilizations as a Self-Fulfilling Prophecy," *European Journal of Social Theory* 9, no. 3 (2006): 316.
24 B. Lance, "Myth, Ritual, and Political Control," in: *Journal of Communication* 30, no. 4 (1980): 166–79.

Where a political myth is well understood it is an easy handrail for officials to use to build consensus. Where is it is not understood, consensus is difficult to build. Violence is often justified in terms of us-them myths, this is because, as Matsumoto and Hwang note, aggression is easier when out-groups are identified and dehumanized, by creating distance between the aggressor, and their society, and the victim.[25] Later chapters will show that the them-us frame features repeatedly in the justifications for violence in modern British political discourse.

Esch suggests that common American war-myths in political culture are *American Exceptionalism* and *Civilisation vs Barbarism*. The first is not directly relevant to Britain, though perhaps *Nostalgic Imperialism* within a wider *Force for Good* is analogous, Colley identified *Force for Good* as an important myth of the elite narrative. This is evident in British war discourse, and performs a similar function to *American Exceptionalism*.[26] The second is a classic version of the them-us paradigm that is often woven into the justification of the use of force. It is evident in much British official discourse, especially regarding terrorism.[27] Myth is used because it appears to work, including playing a role in the public's acceptance of war. Opinion polls pre-Gulf War 1 (1991) show that axiological rhetoric emphasising the evil of Saddam's regime was more compelling than rational arguments.[28] More recently, it is evident throughout the characterisations on the war on terror.[29] Later chapters highlight the use of myth in British war-discourse.

5 Public Opinion, Knowledge and Interest

Public opinion is a very rough measure of public acceptance; public opinion about international affairs is a useful, if not complete, synonym for opinion about the use of force. Brewer et al. note that early investigations concluded that public opinion was unsophisticated and irrational.[30] More recent work

25 D. Matsumoto and H. Hwang, "The Language of political Aggression" in: *Journal of Language and Social Psychology* 32(3) (2012): 337.

26 Colley. "Is Britain a force for good? Investigating British citizens' narrative understanding of war" : 1–22.

27 Esch, "Legitimising the "War on terror"": 358 and 365.

28 B. Rottinghaus, "Presidential Leadership on Foreign Policy, Opinion Polling, and the Possible Limits of 'Crafted Talk'," *Political Communication* 25, no. 2 (2008): 148.

29 Jackson, *Writing the War on Terrorism*: 5.

30 P. Brewer, *et al.* "International Trust and Public Opinion About World Affairs," in: *American Journal of Political Science* 48, no. 1 (2004): 94.

argues that citizens can be rational even if not informed; within this set of heuristics, the concept of political trust was thought to be an important guiding factor.[31] Brunk *et al.*'s findings though were notably reliant on examination of elite attitudes, which therefore omits perhaps the true picture of how the electorate forms attitudes to war. In general, they find that public belief systems are information poor. They find that while public opinion is highly varied and has no central concept to coalesce around,[32] public belief systems provide a coherent and somewhat systematic approach, relying on morals and (political) heuristics, not information, to make decisions regarding support for war.[33] This is instructive because suggests that detailed information is not the ultimate determinant of public opinion. Shea agrees to an extent, public want stories not facts and figures, stories are laced with emotional appeal, and are not just anodyne explanations of events.[34]

There has been an academic focus on how public support for war, rather than an understanding of the realities of war, affects policy, and the Government's perceptions of its own legitimacy. While it would be tempting to use these analyses as proxies for public understanding, it would be wrong to. Mueller concludes, the public often is ignorant of even the most basic aspects of war.[35] Further to this, many of those polled felt underinformed, hinting at the idea that they expected to be able to play an informed role in the democracy.[36] In Britain in 2012, YouGov and Lord Ashcroft found the same, that 69 and 62% respectively of the public felt uninformed of the military's activities.[37] Developing the idea that the public does not use detailed facts to form an understanding of war, Colley argues that an intuitive understanding of war has been built up through public perceptions of Britain's martial and colonial history. Intuition is heavily influenced by social dynamics and bias, meaning that a true, or full, picture of war is rarely held by citizens.[38] This shortfall in understanding is a central concern of this study.

---

31 G. Brunk, D. Secrest, and H. Tamashiro, *Understanding Attitudes about War: modelling moral judgements* (Pittsburgh: University of Pittsburgh Press, 1996).

32 *Ibid.*, 110.

33 *Ibid.*, 49.

34 Shea, interview.

35 J. Mueller, *War, Presidents and Public Opinion* (New York: John Wiley & Sons 1973): 2.

36 *Ibid.*, 112.

37 Royal British Legion, "How much do you know about the Armed Forces?" Last accessed on May 24, 2021 through <www.britishlegion.org.uk/>; Lord Ashcroft, *The Armed Forces and Society;* May 2012 accessed through <www.lordashcroftpolls.com>.

38 Colley, "Is Britain a force for good?": 1–22.

In *Accountability for Killing*, Crawford argues that public neither expresses an interest in, nor exercises oversight of, war. She goes on to say that this does not absolve the public of a responsibility to do so within a democratic framework.[39] For her, war is a social act, the public therefore have a responsibility to oversee it.[40] This is subtly, but importantly, different from the perspective laid out in the Armed Forces Covenant, which suggests that the electorate's role is to *understand* and *support* the executive, not to *scrutinise* or *oversee* decisions and actions.[41] Kasher agrees with Crawford, a democratic government's institutions should be subject to exacting supervision by the public.[42] On the other hand, Laity disagrees and considers scrutiny to be the role of Parliamentarians, who in a representative democracy, as the UK is, are charged with "caring about [war] on behalf of the electorate".[43] Edmund Burke agreed suggesting that elected representatives should be free from the routine opinions of their constituents.[44] But Stewart does not let politicians off the hook, they must be clear in their communication with the public, how else can the public be expected to understand Government policies? Politicians should act as translators of bureaucratic jargon into lay understanding.[45] It is this proposed democratic shortfall that this study explores.

Whether or not the public have an interest in the detail of war, their opinion matters to politicians. But it appears that they overestimate the sensitivity of the public to the costs of violence. Darley and Dandeker argue public are pragmatic and can tolerate considerable levels of violence, politicians should be able to calibrate their communication and policy to this tolerance.[46] YouGov polling showed how insensitive to the costs the UK public can be, there was only a drop from 75% to 64% support for drone strikes by the UK when innocent civilians were *expected* to be killed.[47] Coe argues that this tolerance reflects the clarity of the objectives of the war and the nature of public support; where

39 N. Crawford, *Accountability for Killing: Moral Responsibility for Collateral Damage in Americas Post-9/11 Wars* (New York: Oxford University Press, 2017).

40 *Ibid.*, 422 and 423.

41 United Kingdom, Ministry of Defence, *The Armed Forces Covenant*, 2011.

42 A. Kasher, "Public Trust in a Military Force" in: *Journal of Military Ethics* 2, no 1. (2003): 30.

43 Laity, interview.

44 M. Margolis and G. Mauser, "Public opinion as a Dependent Variable: A Framework for analysis" in: *Political Communication.* 6:2 (1989): 93.

45 Stewart, interview.

46 W. Darley, "War Policy, Public Support, and the Media," in: *Parameters* 35, no. 2 (2005): 127 and C. Dandeker, interview with author, 19 April 2021.

47 De Waal, YouGov, *British attitudes to drones*, YouGov April 3, 2013 accessed through <www.yougov.co.uk>.

objectives are clear and supported, American tolerance for civilian deaths, a proxy measure for violence, is high.[48] It follows that where the political objectives are not clear then tolerance is low. Perhaps obvious, but these are none the less important observations that frame how politicians and officials communicate about war. Van der Meulen adds that trust in the military is central to the tolerance for violence and particularly civilian casualties.[49] Trust is discussed later in the chapter and in the discussion.

6 British Media and Public Authorities

At the heart of the relationship between the media and public authorities lies the tension that the two need each other but are often suspicious of each other's motives. Public authorities are accused of being over-controlling, journalists of treating news as a commodity.[50] But the shape of this relationship is changing, the traditional media is no longer *the* authoritative source it once perhaps was. In *War in 140 Characters,* Patrikarakos, demonstrates how the power of the citizen journalist is replacing it as the key channel for messaging and understanding.[51] Editors will no longer pay for insurance for journalists to visit war zones; Shea highlights how charities and other non-governmental organisations have taken the place as the in-place reporter.[52] As an example of the erosion of reporting on war, the BBC is due to remove its defence correspondent due to financial constraints.[53] It clearly feels the gap can be filled by others. The objective analysis, and explanation, that journalists used to offer the electorate is no longer as accessible as before, and public authorities can no longer rely on them to translate bureaucratic communication on their behalf. The public authorities must communicate directly with the public much more.

Separately, the tenor of war reporting has changed, since the Balkans wars the traditional media has focussed its reporting on the emotional issues surrounding war much more than technical issues. This has influenced official communication and public understanding, as officials now tread carefully around

---

48 K. Coe, "Television News, Public Opinion, and the Iraq War: Do Wartime Rationales Matter?" in: *Communication Research* 40, no. 4 (2013): 488.

49 J. van der Meulen, "Bombing ISIS. Public Support and Public Dilemmas" in: Heereen-Bogers, J. *et al.* (eds.), *The Yin-Yang Military* (Springer, Cham. 2020).

50 J. Seaton, *Carnage and the Media* (Allen Lane: London. 2005): xx.

51 D. Patrikarakos, *War in 140 Characters* (Hachette: New York. 2017).

52 Shea, interview.

53 Laity Twitter, March 19, 2021. Last accessed 8 April 2021.

these emotional triggers, such as civilian deaths, and the public focusses their attention on them.[54] In so doing, Scharrer and Blackburn accuse the media of being complicit in providing sanitised accounts of war.[55] In comparison to Middle Eastern channels, the BBC's editorial guidelines for the showing of violence pay much more Scharrer attention to the sensibilities of the viewer: "We must take care that our journalism does not ... cause unnecessary distress." Al Jazeera do not address violence and harm.[56] Poole makes a strong case of the complicity of the media in sanitising their own violence, in summing up, he quotes Richard Falk, "with the help of the influential media, the state over time has waged and largely won the battle of definitions by exempting its own violence against civilians from being treated as 'terrorism'. Instead, such violence was generally discussed as 'uses of force'".[57]

7 Trust, Transparency, Secrecy

It is in this broad context that trust and transparency are critical to ensuring the Government meets its obligations to *explain* and *justify* its actions so that the public can understand them. Trust and public opinion, while long studied independently, have not been studied together until relatively recently. Hetherington and Globetti argue that trust is used as a heuristic by the public for making political judgements, including about the use of violence, as Brewer et al find in regard to the invasion of Iraq in 2003.[58]

Trust-building is a two-way process that benefits government functioning.[59] Hetherington and Globetti demonstrate this, arguing that in a democracy the public will restrict government activities if they don't trust them, and activities that are unsupervised require more trust from the public. This is particularly the case where the public does not gain an obviously quantifiable benefit or where the public has little personal experience with which to evaluate

54 Laity, interview.

55 E. Scharrer and G. Blackburn, "Images of Injury: Graphic News Visual Effects on Attitudes toward the Use of Unmanned Drones" in: *Mass Communication and Society* 18 (2015): 801.

56 The BBC. *Editorial guidelines,* last accessed May 21, 2021 through <www.bbc.co.uk>; Al Jazeera, *Editorial guidelines*, last accessed May 21, 2021 through <www.allied-media.com>.

57 S. Poole. *Unspeak* (Abacus: London, 2007): 131.

58 Brewer *et al.,* "International Trust and Public Opinion About World Affairs": 93.

59 Whiteley, *et al.*, "Why Do Voters Lose Trust in Governments? Public Perceptions of Government Honesty and Trustworthiness in Britain 2000–2013,": 246.

activity.[60] This is pertinent to the military, whose wars in foreign lands are to a greater degree unsupervised by the public; Kasher argues that most people have limited means to evaluate war, and therefore democratic governments need high levels of trust to have sufficient freedom to operate.[61]

Kasher also argues that transparency is foundational for trust building. He argues that institutions enjoy public trust when the pubic "act towards [them] in accordance with the presumption of [their] proper professional functioning". He then notes that the presumption of proper functioning therefore leads to a presumption of "*proper ethical compliance*" or behaviour. He goes on to describe transparency as central to the presumption of ethical compliance.[62] But the role of transparency is contested, Grimmelikhuijsen *et al* note that some scholars say transparency has no effect at all on trust, while some conclude its can be detrimental. The paper returns to this later.[63]

Turning to secrecy, Thomas argues that politicians manage the inherent paradox that secrecy both protects and endangers democratic self-government. Government arbitrates on the right balance in this paradox, so retains the power in the discourse; in this sense secrecy reproduces elite power.[64] Thomas argues that this undermines the democratic process.[65] Secrecy is particularly alluring in the military context, Carson argues that the temptation to obscure and hide issues is great, as secrecy can buy freedom of action particularly from a dovish society, that politicians are wary of in the UK.[66] The difficulties inherent in the state's use of secrets and sanitised language is similar to that; secrecy and sanitisation are siblings; they both seek to obscure.

60 M. Hetherington, and S. Globetti, "Political Trust and Racial Policy Preferences," in: *American Journal of Political Science* 46, 2 (2002): 254.

61 A. Kasher, "Public Trust in a Military Force": 20–26.

62 *Ibid.*, 42.

63 S. Grimmelikhuijsen, *et al.* "The Effect of Transparency on Trust in Government: A Cross-National Comparative Experiment," in *Public Administration Review* 73, no. 4 (2013): 757.

64 D. Thomas. "Security in the balance: How Britain tried to keep its Iraq War secrets," in: *Security Dialogue* 51. No 1 (2019): 77.

65 *Ibid.*, 84.

66 A. Carson. *Secret Wars: Covert Conflict in International Politics* (2018); USA: Princeton University Press: 298.

CHAPTER 3

Methodology

The research purpose is set out at greater length in the introduction, but in short, this study sees itself as being the foothills of more substantial work to determine whether the British public authorities communicate effectively with the public and what impact this has on Defence and the electorate.

1 Research Objectives

The study had three research objectives:
- To explore Government use of sanitised or opaque language in explaining the use of force/violence to the public.
- To explore whether the use of sanitised or opaque language reduces the understanding of the public *vis-à-vis* violence/force.
- To explore whether sanitised or opaque language creates a (democratic) gap between the public and executive (and military).

2 Position of the Researcher

The position of the researcher as a member of the Armed Forces had both benefits and draw backs for the conduct of the study. Familiarity with the language of violence could have skewed their perceptions,[1] leading to what Neumann calls "home blind", where expressions, practices or structure, abnormal to others are missed and thought of as routine.[2] However being inside the in-group gave the researcher both a degree of credibility with interviewees and cultural competence, having sufficient cultural understanding of an organisation's language to be able to interpret it without losing the nuances of the spoken and unspoken.[3] When dealing with a potentially inflammatory issue being seen as an insider, and therefore potentially less threatening to the institution, was an

1 P. Higate and A. Cameron, "Reflectivity and researching the military" in: *Armed Forces and Society* 32.2 (2006): 221/222.

2 I. Neumann "Discourse Analysis" in: A. Klotz and D. Prakash (eds.), *Qualitative Methods in International Relations* (Palgrave MacMillan: New York. 2008): 65.

3 *Ibid.*, 63.

 | DOI:10.1163/9789004696426_005

advantage for the chief researcher.[4] Bias is implicit in the origin of the study, a personal set of observations; this bias was challenged by interviewees.

3 Armed Forces Covenant – The Experiment Framework

As discussed in Chapter 1, the Armed Forces Covenant provides a framework for electorate-Government relations over the use of force. Much of the focus of the public scrutiny of the Covenant thus far has been about whether the Government upholds its commitments to the Military Community. The commitments to the electorate are less often examined. Therefore, it was the Government's efforts to *justify* and *explain* that this study scrutinised.[5]

4 Research Design and Methods

The study cannot, and does not, give definitive answers but seeks to illuminate and explore the subject matter. The study is concerned with ideas, discourse and tactics evident in communication by the public authorities, in which emotions, perspectives and language are important to the process of creating meaning, understanding and reality.[6] While it attempts to spot trends that might indicate conscious strategies, and correlated impacts, it realises that it is unachievable because of its small sample sizes. Thus, a qualitative discussion was likely to illuminate insights into the nuanced and subjective language used.[7] The study sought to collect data in three areas:

1. *Open-source data.* How is sanitised language used by public authorities: what is said by whom, when, and what does it appear to mean, in what circumstances?
2. *Interviews.* Do officials and journalists recognise the idea of sanitised language and euphemism, why is it used, what impact does it have, what do they think they mean, and what do they think is understood by it?

4 Higate and Cameron, "Reflectivity and researching the military": 228.

5 Ingham, interview.

6 D. Marsh and P. Furlong, "A skin not a sweater: ontology and epistemology in political science," in: V. Lowndes, D. Marsh and G. Stoker, *Theory and methods in political science* (Palgrave MacMillan: New York. 2008): 27.

7 R. Ormston *et al.* "The foundations of qualitative research," in: J. Ritchie (ed.), *Qualitative research practice: a guide for social science students and researchers* (SAGE: Los Angeles, 2014): 16.

3. *Surveys.* How does the public understand the language used by the public authorities? Does the meaning get lost in translation? And how does this impact their support for, and understanding of, the use of violence?

5 Open-Source Data

The study examined official comments available through press releases, press interviews, the media, Parliamentary statements, Parliamentary Committee reports and evidence session. While the list is not exhaustive the range of texts and their different settings allows the study to understand the discourse in the round.[8] Using public information was a great advantage with a contentious subject as it avoided ethical concerns associated with interviewing individuals. However, it meant that the researcher could not directly ask difficult questions, often leaving unanswered the key question of *why* language was used.[9]

These open-source texts were subjected to analysis to discover patterns, linguistic techniques and the relationship between the audience and speaker. Critical discourse analysis investigates how language is used to create, reaffirm, and distribute narratives, values, and perspectives that favour those in power.[10] It helps understand the relationship between language, beliefs, ideology and social and political phenomena. The analysis addressed three broad areas: a description of the text, an interpretation of the text and a subsequent evaluation. The description focusses on lexicographical features, the interpretation seeks to establish what the protagonist was trying to achieve, and the evaluation seeks to place the text in a wider context, assessing its impact.[11]

The study borrows many of Jackson's and Fairclough's questions as a framework for analysis. First, in the description, what is the position of the actors in the sentences, how does sentence construction work to give meaning. Second, what is omitted in the text and how does this impact understanding. And therefore, what prior knowledge is assumed, can be reasonably assumed, and how might this alter understanding of the audience; can the speaker hide behind the ignorance of the reader? What meanings are given explicitly to terms, and

8 Neumann, "Discourse Analysis": 67.

9 J. Lewis and C. Nicholls, "Design Issues", in: J. Ritchie (ed.), *Qualitative research practise: a guide for social science students and researchers*: 57.

10 K. O' Halloran, "Critical Discourse Analysis," in: J. Simpson (ed.), *The Routledge Handbook of Applied Linguistics* (Routledge: Abingdon. 2011): 445.

11 I. Fairclough and N. Fairclough, *Political Discourse Analysis: A method for advanced students* (Routledge: Abingdon. 2012): 90.

what meanings are left implicit in the reading? What is implied by the text, its context and therefore how does this alter the understanding of the reader? In this context how else could clarity be given, and what are the risks associated with this for the speaker, and perhaps for the reader? Further to these questions, it was also important to examine texts as a whole, how do different parts of the texts relate to each other, and how does this shape the understanding of the reader?

The context of the texts is important. The following is not a full list but gives an impression of important issues. First, the position audience and speaker relative to one another, exposing the nature of their relationship, particularly the power dynamic. Second, the historical context that shapes the interpretation of the reader and the phrasing of the speaker. Third, contemporary context shapes audience and speaker. Fourth, how language is reinforced by other discursive actions, this could include policy. What is the interplay between language and action? What is the impact of this normalisation? Fifth, the role communications channels play, in particular translators, reinforcers, or critics.[12]

6 Interviews

Semi-structured interviews were used to paint a picture beyond what was available through open source. It was understood early on that a collecting information from a truly representative sample would not be achievable, however the interviews were important in challenging assumptions and biases held by the researcher and opening up avenues of exploration that were otherwise blind spots. Convenience sampling was used, recognising that this meant quantitative data would not be available for analysis, that the observations would not necessarily reflect wider opinion, and there could be ethical challenges.[13]

Interviewees were approached if they had a role in the explanation of violence to the electorate, or relevant academic credentials. Interviewee cohorts included: those who had a role in creating official language or messaging, such as media departments; those whose message was being communicated, such as senior officials; those who had a role in interpreting or translating the message for the electorate, such as journalists; and academics who have worked

12 Jackson, *Writing the War on Terrorism*: 24; Fairclough and Fairclough, *Political Discourse Analysis:* 76–116.

13 J. Brewis, "The ethics of researching friends: on convenience sampling in qualitative management and organisation studies," in: *British Journal of Management:* 25 (2014): 859–861.

alongside the military. Despite the potentially challenging discussions the interviews could throw up, most were happy to be on the record. It was recognised that those serving within public authorities may have been concerned about speaking up "against" the institution.[14] Despite the small sample, a number of the interviewees can be considered as experts in their particular fields, see bibliography for details.

Interviews were semi-structured with similar initiating questions designed to allow a flowing discussion that could be steered into the interviewees' area of expertise. Though not explicit in all cases, the researcher used a Likert scale to understand the strength of opinion around the issues, similar to the methods used by Brunk *et al.*[15] Questions were both abstract in nature, to consider general arguments, and also specific, to add colour to the discussion. Questions addressed how military activity should be scrutinised or overseen in the UK, whether there was a difference between the framework for scrutiny and the reality of it.

7 Limitations and Trustworthiness

In summary there are two key issues. First, the small sample sizes make drawing definitive conclusions difficult, however, the observations made do indicate areas worthy of more detailed examination. Second, time and resources prevented the study from surveying electorate opinion and understanding of the issue, so conclusions rely on proxy arguments.

---

14 *Ibid.*, 860.

15 Brunk *et al.*, *Understanding Attitudes about War.*

CHAPTER 4

Findings

This chapter analyses two cases that highlight the use of sanitised language by the public authorities in *justifying* and *explaining* the use violence. Those are: operations in Libya, operations against the so-called Islamic State. The paper also briefly considers a report into the UK's use of drones by the Joint Committee on Human Rights Select Committee. Much of the discussion rests on the specifics of the use of violence and particularly efforts to obscure the costs of war to the electorate: human, financial and political. Each case study has key protagonists, narrative and context that are set out before official language is examined in detail. In Libya and Iraq, UK appears to adopt techniques associated with "surrogacy". The UK followed a no boots on the ground policy, rather choosing to support local forces who do the fighting on the ground. The UK deployed unmanned air vehicles, or drones, as well as manned aircraft, to the theatres. The Government's narratives included the idea the conflict did not cost the public much. Themes illuminated by the research are discussed in the next chapter, but the linguistic techniques that are prominent include: euphemism, abstract language, separation of the speaker from the actions on the ground, dehumanisation of the enemy and flattening of interest and emotion.

1 Libya Introduction

Prime Minister David Cameron led the UK into the NATO 2011 intervention into Libya. The study also looks at statements by Secretary of State for Defence Dr Liam Fox, the UK Permanent Representative to the UN, Sir Mark Lyall Grant, and UK Permanent Representative to NATO's North Atlantic Council, Marriot Leslie. Later interventions in Libya see another Secretary of State for Defence, Sir Michael Fallon, give interviews. Regime change, civilian deaths and post-conflict activity proved to be areas where public authorities sanitised language.

2 Overarching Narrative

Cameron's argument for UK intervention in Libya was complex and multifaceted. Within this, humanitarian grounds for intervention were an important aspect of the story the British Government told the public. The fight against Gaddafi was billed as an effort to protect civilians who were caught in the battle between forces seeking the removal of Gaddafi and forces loyal to him.[1] This was an explicit purpose of United Nations Security Council Resolution (UNSCR) 1973.[2] Much of the UK's narrative saw UK national interest as secondary to the protection of civilian life. This had consequences for how the campaign could be conducted and therefore spoken about. The need to reduce the human costs to the civilians on the ground, and also to the UK, was central to legitimacy and support at home. This, and the framing of Gaddafi as barbaric, was at the core of the narrative of the war; UK action was limited to bombing in support of anti-Gaddafi forces.[3] Fox said, "I argued … [we had to show] we had to place a higher regard for the lives of civilians … than the regime that was being replaced."[4] NATO countries portrayed Gaddafi as the "barbaric other". Cameron said "there was urgent need to … stop [Gaddafi's] *slaughter* [of civilians]."[5] The language used to *justify* the war was clear. The language used for *explaining* NATO's actions, particularly contentious or politically damaging action was much less clear.

3 Regime Change

UNSCR 1973 did not allow regime change, but NATO was accused of pursuing it. Lyall Grant, rejected the accusation when questioned by the House of Commons Defence Select Committee "we have not been aiming, through this resolution and through the military action, at regime change."[6]

None the less, accusations persisted, the Government was forced into awkward exchanges. In late March, Cameron said "We have a situation in Libya, whereby there was a dictator whose people were trying to get rid of him",[7] provoking understandable concerns that regime change was indeed a NATO

1 T. Colley, "What's in it for us? Responses to the UK's strategic narrative on intervention in Libya," in *The RUSI Journal*, 160.4 (2015): 60.

2 United Nations, *United Nations Security Council Resolution 1973* (17 March 2011): 1.

3 Colley, "What's in it for us?": 63, 65.

4 *The Guardian*, 'David Cameron's Libya War: why the PM felt Gaddafi had to be stopped,' (2 October 2011).

5 *Ibid.*

6 United Kingdom, *House of Commons Defence Select Committee Ninth Report-Operations in Libya* (25 January 2012): 33, <www.data.parliament>.

7 United Kingdom, *Hansard House of Commons Debate* (21 March 2011): Column 708, <www.hansard.parliament.uk>.

objective. Fox said "I would have thought that a very clear aim for us is that the free decision of people to determine their own future is something we would want to see ... it was self-evident. But it is clear that regime change would be a major policy objective, and one that is not signed up to in the Resolution [1973]."[8] It is easy to see how commentators and public may have seen this distinction as false, or at least have been suspicious of it; explanations of NATO actions were often opaque, particularly when it came to the direct targeting of Gaddafi and his family. Both Lyall Grant and Fox acknowledged that if Gaddafi and other members of his government were present in military establishments, such as command and control centres, they could be killed. Lyall Grant set out the legal argument "of course there are circumstances when, if you can make [the killing of Gaddafi] link to the protection of civilians, that military action is justified."[9]

In a session of evidence to the Defence Select Committee, Fox answered questions about the alleged direct targeting of Gaddafi and his inner circle. He summarised the position "If some of the individuals whom we regarded as leaders of the regime happened to be [where we chose to bomb], that was their tough luck. *We targeted capabilities, not the individuals*."[10] This is militarily accurate, command and control capabilities were targeted, these consisted of communications systems, physical locations from where commanders could command, but necessarily it also includes military commanders. While recognising that Fox is attempting to make a specific point to rebuff allegations of illegal direct targeting of Gaddafi, he reinforces the common dehumanising narrative that capabilities are distinct from individuals. Further to this, Fox relies on the audience having sufficient prior understanding of military terminology and procedures to be able to see that there is a distinction between the specific point he is making and the general. In general, targeting command and control capabilities means killing commanders as well as preventing them from communicating effectively with their troops.

4 Civilian Casualties

The prospect of civilian casualties was of great concern to the UK. While these were not a cost borne by the public in the UK, they were a political cost for UK and Alliance politicians, who had framed the mission more in terms of civilian

8 *House of Commons Defence Select Committee Ninth Report-Operations in Libya:* 31.

9 *Ibid.*, 33.

10 *Ibid.*

safety than direct national interest. The Government argued strongly that Britain was very careful in its approach to bombing in Libya, avoiding civilian casualties where ever possible, often privileging civilian life over military progress.[11] Fox was explicit in his evidence to the Defence Select Committee: "we must at all times minimise the chance of civilian casualties."[12] But achieving this was not easy, and allegations of civilian deaths caused by NATO were reported.[13]

A good example of how the public authorities sanitised civilian deaths was given by Marriot Leslie, who set out the challenges that NATO faced in avoiding civilian casualties.

> You then cannot see inside every single building to be absolutely sure that a shard of glass has not gone through somebody you cannot see, *so you cannot say with honesty and certainty 'I know for a fact that I have not killed a civilian'. We do not know that we have, and* we believe that there would be very few, if we have [killed any civilians] at all.[14]

Leslie begins by being very clear that it is virtually impossible to understand the scale of potential or actual civilian casualties and deaths, but then in the second sentence asserts that NATO believes that there were few casualties if NATO had indeed killed anyone at all. While the contradictory nature of this position appears obvious, the phrase "to be absolutely sure that a shard of class has not gone through somebody you cannot see" makes the notion of being able to account for deaths absurd. There is a clear effort to disassociate NATO bombing into dense urban areas from civilian casualties, and in so doing sanitising NATO actions.

5 Post-campaign

Post-NATO-campaign Libya presented the UK with two major challenges, development and terrorism. In response to a Select Committee question about moving from the war to rebuilding the country, Fox says "nothing would please us more than for the *kinetic element* to be over."[15] Fox uses euphemism, *kinetic*

11 *The Guardian*, 'David Cameron's Libya War'.

12 *House of Commons Defence Select Committee – Minutes of Evidence HC 950.*

13 *New York Times*, 'Scores of unintended casualties in NATO war in Libya' (18 December 2011), <www.nytimes.com>.

14 *House of Commons Defence Select Committee Ninth Report-Operations in Libya*: 36.

15 *House of Commons Defence Select Committee – Minutes of Evidence HC 950.*

element instead of bombing campaign, or war, obscuring NATO's responsibility for the damage and suffering. Fox uses the passive voice and nominalisation (swapping of a noun for a verb – kinetic element for bombing), to further remove NATO from the consequences of their actions – *the kinetic element to be over*. He could have said, "when we stop bombing". Fox then moves swiftly to the active voice and takes responsibility for NATO actions that are much more palatable to most domestic audiences "(nothing would please us more than) ... for *us* [NATO] to be able to focus on UN assistance to the *humanitarian effort*".[16] The reader is left wondering whose kinetic element will be over, while admiring NATO's contribution to the humanitarian effort. Of course, NATO was complicit in both.

Later, European countries and the US became concerned with the rise of terrorist organisations in Libya. A Deash affiliate organisation grew in southern Libya and was attacked by forces supported by the US and UK. On 19 February 2016 US aircraft took off from the UK and bombed a training camp, where the US believed Noureddeine Chouchane was located. Chouchane was suspected of being involved in recent attacks in Tunisia, including in Sousse where 30 Britons had been killed.[17] The Secretary of State for Defence had to authorise the use of British bases for the US attack. Answering questions about the attack, Fallon said:

> I welcome this strike that *has taken out a Daesh training camp* being used to train terrorists to carry out attacks. I was satisfied that *its destruction* makes us all safer, and I personally authorised the US use of our bases.[18]

De-humanisation is the central lexical device in this passage, Fallon makes no mention of the individual who was the actual target of the attack, nor any of the other potential Daesh fighters that were killed. Fallon uses the *training camp* as the subject of the attack, and uses the passive voice, which disassociate the reader from the reality of the attack, though later he uses the active to show solidarity and strength, presumably for public approval (*"I personally authorised"*). 41 people were killed and the US could not confirm if the principal target of the attack, Chouchane, was among them.[19] Fallon does not discuss these aspects of the attack. By placing it as the subject, the *training camp*

16 *Ibid.*

17 *The Guardian,* 'US airstrikes target Islamic State militants in Libya,' (19 February 2016), <www.theguardian.com>.

18 *Ibid.*

19 *Ibid.*

takes the place of the undisclosed 41 dead in the minds of the reader, it is the *training camp* that presented a threat to the UK. The *training camp* was a set of simple buildings and tents in the desert, which did not themselves present a threat to the UK. The actual lasting effect was achieved by killing the suspected members of Daesh in the camp. In addition, because he uses *training camp* as the subject, Fallon can further sanitise the event by using the phrase *taken out*, having therefore the effect of disconnecting the reader from the human reality of war.

6 Iraq and Syria – Counter Daesh Coalition

Prime Minister David Cameron and his Secretary of State for Defence, Sir Michael Fallon were key domestic communicators regarding the fight against the so-called Islamic State or Deash. They were supported by a cast of senior officers, including Deputy Chief of Defence Staff (Military Strategy and Operations), responsible for Defence's missions and operations. The Ministry of Defence communicated as an institution through written evidence to Parliamentary Select Committees and press statements.

7 Overarching Narrative

Despite the ignominious background of war in Iraq, the Coalition fight against the so-called Islamic State, or Daesh, was supported.[20] The enemy was billed as barbaric, and the Coalition as noble. In addressing the House of Commons regarding the UK and US killing of Britons Junaid Hussain and Reyaad Khan on 7 September 2015, Cameron said, "the threat-the *poisonous* ideology of Islamist extremism" and going on to say, "Both Junaid Hussain and Reyaad Khan were ... seeking to orchestrate *specific* and *barbaric* attacks against the west".[21]

But Cameron did not want to shoulder the burden of war. The following short passage set the scene for future engagements by others, Cameron said in Parliament:

---

20 W. Dahlgreen, ISIS: How 57% came to favour air strikes (YouGov. 26 September 2014), <www. yougov.co.uk>.

21 United Kingdom, *Hansard House of Commons Debate* (7 September 2015): Column 25, <www.hansard.parliament.uk>.

> we do not need ground troops to target the supply of oil which Daesh uses to fund terrorism. We do not need ground troops to hit Daesh's headquarters, its infrastructure, its supply routes, its training facilities, its weapons supplies.[22]

Cameron is unequivocal that the UK does not need to bear the emotional costs, UK deaths, of the war to be successful – *we do not need ground troops*. Cameron then goes on to use abstraction and sanitization, *hitting headquarters ... facilities*, omitting the consequence that the UK would be killing those inside the facilities. Others followed his lead.

In written evidence to the House of Commons Defence Select Committee, responding to a question on the number of attacks conducted by the Royal Air Force (RAF) in support of their partners on the ground, Fallon uses a construction whose inferred message is designed to confirm the UK (and Coalition's) position as the responsible actors in the war, and to disconnect the electorate from the costs of war.

> I would stress that neither the UK nor the Coalition is undertaking a generalised bombing campaign in Syria ... Rather the Coalition, including the RAF, is giving targeted air support to specific counter-Daesh offensives.[23]

Fallon juxtaposes activities with negative connotations, which the UK is not involved in, against those with positive associations, which the UK is. The RAF does not bomb enemy soldiers, it *gives air support* to friendly soldiers. Bombing is understood, it leads to death and destruction. On the other hand, *giving air support* to a friendly force is a positive action. Further, the use of *air support* conceals the fact that some of this also results in death and destruction on the ground, precisely where Daesh are, and British boots are not. While Fallon is probably trying to communicate that British attacks are carefully considered, through this de-humanisation of UK activity (*air support*), the electorate is disconnected from the costs of war and the reality that is faced by those living in the warzone, upon whom the costs are exacted in the name of the electorate.

---

22 United Kingdom, *Hansard House of Commons Debate* (2 December 2015): Column 332, <www.hansard.parliament.uk>.

23 United Kingdom, Written evidence for *House of Commons Defence Select Committee Report: UK Military Operations in Syria and Iraq* (16 September 2016), <www.publication.parliament.uk>.

8 Killing to Success?

The US Secretary for Defence, General James Mattis, declared that the Coalition was following a policy of *annihilation* of Daesh.[24] A lay person's understanding annihilation involves killing, and destruction of equipment and institutions.[25] While this sort of rhetoric, and perhaps strategy, appeals to the US domestic audiences, it is much more problematic in the UK, however much it might be the reality.[26] It is in this context that UK ministers had to discuss Coalition strategy.

In providing evidence for the Defence Select Committee, Fallon, when pressed on the nature of the airstrikes and the numbers of Daesh killed by the Royal Air Force and Coalition, said that:

> Let me start by saying it is extremely misleading to look at statistics in that particular way … the aim of these missions is not to kill as many Daesh as possible, but to degrade them on occasions by tackling their leadership and in the end to try to undermine their will to fight by attacking their command and control, their infrastructure and so on. It is far too simplistic to simply measure a mission by the number of people killed. As you are implying, many of the missions are to gather intelligence rather than to inflict casualties. The pre-planned missions are usually targeted at infrastructure.[27]

In the second clause Fallon sets up the *mission* as the subject of the sentence, not the forces doing the mission. This creates a degree of separation between the actual doer, the RAF, from the consequences of the thing that has been done, the mission. Further, there has been nominalisation, in this case "bombing" has been swapped for "mission", which associates the concrete action of bombing with the more abstract concept of a mission, which is not defined, and removes the need to a subject to do the bombing. This reduces the potential negative consequences of the mission in the mind of the reader.

24 F. Solomon, "Defence Chief James Mattis says the US is using 'annihilation tactics' against ISIS" (Time, May 29, 2017), <www.time.com>.

25 <www.dictionary.cambridge.org>.

26 Shea, interview.

27 United Kingdom, Oral evidence for *House of Commons Defence Select Committee Report: UK Military Operations in Syria and Iraq* (26 May 2016), <www.publication.parliament.uk>.

In trying again to demonstrate that British attacks are well thought through, Fallon uses clear language to say what UK forces will not do – *kill* or measure the number of people *killed* – but becomes abstract when referring to what UK forces will do: *degrade … by tackling … leadership, command and control … targeted at infrastructure*. Also, noteworthy are the omissions from the passage, while *many of the missions are to gather intelligence rather than to inflict casualties,* there are clearly missions that are in fact specifically designed to inflict casualties.

Giving evidence to the same inquiry, again about the nature of the UK's airstrikes, the Deputy Chief of Defence Staff (DCDS) described the difference between the approach taken by the UK in Iraq and Syria. In evidence he says: "in Syria the object is *to disrupt command and control* and *interdict and disrupt lines of communication*". He set out that in Iraq the strategy was to ensure "*tactical overmatch*".[28]

While the DCDS quite properly uses technical military terms, as a military professional, to describe the actions of those he is responsible for, he fails to translate them into easily understandable language for the layperson. In relying on technical language, he does not explain the situation to the Committee, what exactly does *tactical overmatch* mean in the field?

Later he describes how the use of air power is affecting Daesh: "there are a particular number of target sets … *the ability of the caliphate* to *command and control itself* … tackle its finances and reduce liquidity … [we seek to] destroy some of its critical infrastructure."

By using the term *Caliphate* as a catch all for the people, infrastructure and ideology, the DCDS sanitises the impacts of war. This physical and conceptual entity, a patch of land and an identity, the Caliphate, takes on the responsibilities of the human leadership that runs the Caliphate, and in so doing dehumanising them. Violence is inflicted on a concept not people. Further, the *Caliphate* does not in fact *command and control itself*, people of the caliphate command and control other people of the Caliphate. This construction creates a very abstract concept of command and control, when the reality for the RAF is that it is concrete, real, tangible. People and communications systems are bombed, killed and destroyed.

Further to this, in written evidence to the Defence Select Committee, the Ministry of Defence wrote:

28 *Ibid.*

> The Coalition has now moved into the degrade phase of the campaign. ... both in Iraq and Syria, Coalition airpower is being applied to diminish Daesh numbers and morale; to degrade its ability to manoeuvre by destroying vehicles and by raising the costs of open movement; to destroy defensive positions and materiel stocks; to prevent resupply to forward positions; to isolate elements from leadership structures; to eliminate senior leaders.[29]

The first clause can be somewhat excused for beginning with an anodyne description, *the degrade phase*, as it follows the military terminology, the Coalition had progressed onto the "Degrade Phase" in its plan of action. But the explanation that follows should give the Committee a sense of the reality, this is after all what the Committee is investigating; but it does not. First, *airpower* takes the most prominent role in the sentence, it is an abstract concept. Who exactly is the Coalition's *airpower*, and how can they be held accountable? These questions go unanswered. The author uses the passive voice (*is being applied*) further removing the real, hidden, subject, the pilots and senior officers of the Coalition, from the consequences of their actions. Then in one of the clearest uses of abstraction as a tool, members of Daesh are de-humanised, reduced to being *numbers* who are *diminished*, and further sanitized by the addition of *morale*, which is elevated to sit alongside (undeclared) human lives. This clause could read "the RAF is killing members of Daesh", but the author did not write it in this fashion, the political burdens would lie clearly with the UK if they had written it thus. The short statement "*degrade its ability to manoeuvre* by destroying vehicles and *raising the costs of open movement*" is another example of how abstraction reduces impact, this too could be re-written to say, "the RAF will kill members of Daesh if they try to move from one place to another and destroy their vehicles".

There are instances where the Government is somewhat more explicit, though even here there is evidence of abstraction. In an official MOD report, a justification for set of RAF attacks in Mosul in 2017 precedes short descriptions of what happened. The justification reads: "[the RAF] were able to provide *invaluable air support. Without this, Iraqi forces would have been unable to re-take Mosul*".[30] The reader is unable to challenge the assertion here, there is no counter-factual available. Was the RAF really invaluable? Could the Iraqis

29 United Kingdom, Ministry of Defence, *Memorandum submitted by the Ministry of Defence* for *House of Commons Defence Select Committee Report: UK Military Operations in Syria and Iraq* (1 December 2015), <www.data.parliament.uk>.

30 *Warfare Today*, "RAF plays its Part in re-taking Mosul," <www.warfare.today.com> (10 July 2017).

not have re-taken Mosul? Could no other Coalition member have fulfilled this role? Understandably, the report continues to frame the contribution the RAF attacks make as positive "*invaluable*" and "*in very close support of Iraqi forces*".

The report then moves to detailing the attacks, in common with other descriptions of attacks by UK forces, the report uses abstract terms to describe the events on the ground. *Targets* were hit, these included *groups* and *teams* that are more descriptive of human sacrifice than is common with public announcement, but these are qualified by reinforcing the barbarism of the intended human target, the *terrorist*, inoculating the reader from concern for them. But there is little consistency, the report continues later with again more de-humanising and abstract language, "[The RAF conducted] *pinpoint attacks on a pair of firing positions* where *the terrorists had stationed a recoilless anti-tank rifle and a machine gun*."[31] In this sentence the attacks were on the *firing points* not the people (and perhaps they were on empty buildings). The consequence of the attacks has been omitted, was there just a pile of rubble? Or were the members of Daesh killed? The use of the expression *pinpoint* is designed to conjure notions of professional competence and care for civilians, to reinforcing the overarching narrative.

9 General Human Rights – Drones

The Joint Committee on Human Rights Select Committee examined the UK's use of drones, in the wake of the killing the aforementioned Khan and Hussain. The title of the report is striking: *The Government's policy on the use of drones for targeted killing*. It uses the word *killing* in a way that the Government themselves are reticent to, and it makes explicit the fact that there is a policy of doing so, not something that is as obvious in Government statements. The report is an interesting comparison in the use of language in the UK discourse.[32]

The Government was understandably wary of charges of *targeted killing* as it sounds very much like assassination, which is illegal. The answers given by the Government, when challenged as to whether there is a policy of targeted killing are contradictory. Fallon, appeared initially to be unequivocal in his oral evidence, declaring, "*There is no policy of targeting killing*". However, when challenged whether in similar circumstances there would be similar actions undertaken, he replied:

31 *Ibid.*

32 United Kingdom, *Joint Committee on Human Rights: The Government's policy on the use of drones for targeted killing*, 27 April 2016, <www.publications.parliament.uk>.

> If there is a direct and imminent threat to the United Kingdom and there is no other way of dealing with it – it is not possible to interdict that threat or arrest or detain people involved in that threat – then of course as a last resort we have to use force.[33]

This statement demonstrates the conditions in which the Government would make the same decision repeatedly. This repetition might appear to constitute policy. The Joint Committee also found this to be the case and concluded that

> despite the sometimes confusing explanations offered by the Government. … It is clear that the Government does have a policy to use lethal force abroad outside armed conflict.[34]

These exchanges are worth considering because even without the emotional and political implications associated with the setting of specific campaigns or wars, Fallon cannot bring himself to use the word *kill* unless forced to. In the passage above, he substitutes *kill* with *force*, despite the line of questioning being specifically about killing. Fallon only uses *kill* when specifically rebuffing the charge that there is a policy of *targeted killing*, which appears contradictory. The Government is usually at pains to demonstrate that the killings it sanctions are in fact highly targeted, they are as we have seen *pinpoint*, and aimed at specific not general *targets*. While to the military or legal expert the contradictions may be important distinctions in law, they go to show how little clarity there is for the lay person.

10 Trends?

The evidence appears to show two trends in these cases, first that the language used to justify action was typically clear and emotive, designed to persuade the electorate. The second that explanation of "home team" use of violence is often deliberately laced with sanitising language. Communication about other recent conflicts show signs of similar language, but there is not space to address them here. The next chapter discusses these findings.

---

33 United Kingdom, *Oral evidence for Joint Committee on Human Rights: The Government's policy on the use of drones for targeted killing*, 16 December 2015, <www.publications.parliament.uk>.

34 United Kingdom, *The Government's policy on the use of drones for targeted killing*: 37.

CHAPTER 5

Discussion

The discussion now turns to whether the use of sanitising language is a modern phenomenon, or whether it was ever thus. It then explores factors that influence the use of sanitising language, before making comments on its potential impact.

1 Was It Ever Thus?

It is possible to be clear about the use of violence in controversial circumstances that might incentivise the use of sanitised language. At the end of World War 2, the British Government maintained that bombing whole German cities was required despite questions as to whether it was necessary and proportionate given the trajectory of the war and impact to civilians. Rather than being an unfair comparison to Libya or Iraq, it is precisely because the circumstances and language surrounding the bombing are so different that it draws out useful observations; it is valuable because it forces one to consider an alternative, perhaps extreme, perspective.

Lord Cecil, Secretary of State for Dominion Affairs, in answering questions in the House, used highly descriptive language "the purpose of these *intensive [Allied] attacks upon German cities* is ... to bring to a standstill enemy war production, and not merely ... with the object of ... spreading fear among the civilian population." However, despite being direct and clear about the activity, Cecil employs similar techniques as modern politicians to flatten the prominence of the negative consequences of the bombing. Later in the passage though Cecil returns to being direct on the subject of violence "*we* should face hard facts frankly ... The hard, inescapable fact is that war is a horrible thing and that it cannot be carried on without suffering, often to those who are not immediately responsible for causing the conflict. ... *We cannot expect to find a means of conducting hostilities which do not involve suffering*."[1] Cecil places the Government as the subject, taking responsibility for the impacts of the bombing, and is clear that it causes suffering. This is different to British Government

1 United Kingdom, *Hansard House of Commons Debate* (9 February 1944): Column 737, <www.hansard.parliament.uk>.

communication about the 2011 Libya and counter-Daesh campaigns. In another demonstration of the Government's commitment to the policy and the associated costs, The Secretary of State for Air, Sir Archibald Sinclair, responded to a goading question "*if I were* allowed to choose only one target [for bombing] in Germany, the target *I should choose* would be Berlin."[2] It is clear therefore that under different circumstances the language can be different.

The modern use of sanitising language jars with the general trend of Government communication which has, at least in theory, been towards transparency. Certainly since Tony Blair's leadership, the British Government has recognised the need to keep the public informed (communicative not strategic language) and has played a leading role in publicising its own affairs.[3] This is manifested in legislation, requiring Government departments to inform the public of their activities and costs. As discussed in Chapter 1, the Armed Forces Act 2011 is one such piece of legislation. The Defence Select Committee tries to hold the Government to account for this in its report *Operations in Iraq and Syria*:

> if the Government is to continue to justify and validate its policy of airstrikes in Syria, it should provide the necessary detail on what is being targeted. We therefore recommend that the MoD put this information, as far as possible, into the public domain so that realistic judgements on the effectiveness of the UK's air operations in Syria can be made.[4]

They use language that is markedly different to the Government's. The Committee choses to draw a distinction between "collateral damage" and "civilian casualties", a step towards re-humanising the war in official public discourse.[5] The former refers to inadvertent damage to infrastructure and materiel, the latter to injured and killed civilians.

Further to this, perhaps in recognition that there is an unhealthy knowledge-gap between the electorate and the Government, the newly released Integrated Review, which signals the UK's strategic priorities for the coming decade,

2 United Kingdom, *Hansard House of Commons Debate* (1 December 1943): Vol 395, <www.hansard.parliament.uk>.

3 B. Maartens, "From Propaganda to 'Information': Reforming Government Communications in Britain," in: *Contemporary British History* 30:4 (2016): 556.

4 House of Commons Defence Select Committee: *Report UK Military Operations in Syria and Iraq*: para. 75.

5 *Ibid.*, para. 58.

includes "strategic communications and public engagement capability" as a priority for reform.[6]

It is no surprise that concern with the clarity of public discourse is echoed across the press.[7] Parris specifically addressed the issue in 2009 for *The Times*, when he argued "It's easy to be blinded by the valiant effort, as well as the acronyms and euphemisms. But the harsh truth does not change." He goes on to say: "Language says so much. The acronyms and buzz phrases tell you of a crazy paving of assistance and command ... it tells of baffled expatriates and aid workers ... in flight from reality."[8]

2 What Do These Comparisons Tell Us?

As becomes clear on reading Fussell's anthology, *The Bloody Game,* each period has its own language.[9] So, what accounts for the differences between the language used in World War 2 and Iraq-Counter Daesh or Libya 2011? The first strand of argument draws on Clausewitz, who says that war is the "province of social life", it reflects the domestic society and culture that the protagonists hail from.[10] It follows therefore that the use of language by the public authorities is not necessarily deliberately sanitising, rather it reflects trends evident elsewhere in society. Sanitising of the language of war is consistent with a (contested) wider reduction in levels and acceptance of violence in domestic society, the societal taboo on speaking about death, and de-legitimisation of the use of violence for foreign and security policy, particularly in the wake of the 2003 Iraq invasion.[11] Within this context, the wide use of euphemism in society demonstrates its value. But this is the domain of socially, not politically, constructed euphemism; communicative euphemism, not strategic euphemism, remains socially acceptable, and to an extent necessary.[12] There

6 United Kingdom, Ministry of Defence, *Global Britain in a competitive age: The integrated Review of Security, Defence, Development and Foreign Policy* (2021): 97.

7 Interviews with author, D. Loyn, May 3; S. Joshi, April 21; K. Sengupta, May 10; R. Fox, May 14, 2021.

8 M. Parris, 'In the fog, remember: victory is impossible in Afghanistan,' *The Times*, 4 July 2009 <www.thetimes.co.uk>.

9 P. Fussell (ed.), *The Bloody Game: An Anthology of Modern War* (Scribners: London. 1991).

10 C. Coker personal communications and C. Coker, *War in an age of risk* (Polity: Cambridge. 2009): 32.

11 J. Gray, "Steven Pinker is wrong about violence and war" *The Guardian,* May 13, 2015, <www.theguardian.com>.

12 K. Burridge, *Is political correctness a euphemism for euphemism?* (1999), <www.abc.net> 7 May 2021.

is great temptation to use strategic euphemism as it is highly effective. Times Mirror polling showed that 21% of people were concerned about the "collateral damage" produced by the Persian Gulf War in contrast to the 49% who worried about the "civilian casualties and other unintended damage".[13] Given that Governments must do what they think is right, but must also be re-elected, Laity argues that avoiding confrontation with the public is sufficient political incentive to explain the use of "de-colourised" or abstract language.[14]

In addition, science has had a profound influence on modern culture, and therefore the practise and language of war. As Bousquet says "The most visible impact of these technologies on the world may be their material imprint but this should not obscure their profound cultural impact, enmeshed as they are in contemporaneous discourses whether, scientific, philosophical, or other."[15] Discourse of war reflects this move from ideas of human and existential war to scientific and instrumental, it is littered with the language of systems, networks and cost-benefit analyses.

Responding to these social conditions, the public authorities' confidence to use direct language, perhaps unsurprisingly, appears to correlate with public support for war. The Second World War had a coherent and supported narrative of national security; it was easily *justified* because the threat to either the UK, or to another, was clear and present in the minds of the electorate.[16] Language around the sinking of the Belgrano in the Falklands War, another well supported action based on national security, was similarly blunt.[17] This broad base of support gave public authorities the freedom to *explain* their actions clearly. On the other hand, the British Government's justification for the 2011 Libya campaign was multi-faceted and contested,[18] and though the campaign against Daesh was well supported, British action in Iraq had an ignominious recent history, making it difficult ground to cover for politicians.[19] It appears that where links to national security are difficult to explain, sanitised language is frequently used.

13 Norris, "Military Censorship and the Body Count in the Persian Gulf War": 231.

14 Laity, interview.

15 A. Bousquet, *The Scientific Way of Warfare: Order and Chaos on the Battlefields of Modernity*, (Hurst & Co: London. 2009): 239.

16 M. Smith, "Jeremy Corbyn is on the right side of public opinion about foreign policy: except for the Falklands," YouGov. May 30, 2017, <www.yougov.com>.

17 United Kingdom, Houses of Parliament, *Hansard* vol 23. May 4, 1982, <www.api.parliament.uk>.

18 Colley, "What's in it for us?".

19 Dahlgreen, *ISIS: How 57% came to favour air strikes;* Chilcot, *The Iraq inquiry.*

Looking at the political aspects of this more closely, Kaldor argues human security is the dominant driver for modern Western war, not national, security.[20] The individual is challenging the collective as the political unit of measure in the UK, and other European liberal democracies, but it has not yet won out. The notion of human security has developed alongside this phenomenon.[21] Governments *justify* wars in terms of human security, as in Libya 2011 and Counter Daesh Iraq, and therefore feel they cannot be seen to harm individuals. The fact that less than 50% of the public support military intervention on humanitarian grounds adds to the pressure to keep these wars clean.[22] As a result, militaries now make considerable efforts to hide the emotional costs of war, necrology is a key battleground, the suppression of own dead and dehumanisation of the enemy is designed to induce a more favourable, or at least a less unfavourable, public response to war.[23] This becomes particularly evident as the peace dividend of the Cold War is realised, Shea and Laity both identify the Balkans as a moment at which the trend of the UK's narrative of war changes, epitomised by the Responsibility to Protect doctrine.[24] The UK military responded to this shift which challenged the value of violence as an instrument of policy, in public at least. The UK set up the Permanent Joint Headquarters in 1996; reflecting their interpretation of the new political context, staff officers and commanders deliberately sanitised language to demonstrate the military's relevance to the emerging (less violent) political environment.[25] This non-confrontational language was perhaps also designed to fit in better with British decision-making culture, which Kenneth Walz describes as "[seeking] to dampen conflicts and depreciate dangers, to compromise rather than fight, to postpone decisions, to obscure issues rather than confront them".[26]

Sanitised language became internal jargon and remains part of the internal discourse. Seely and Loyn argue that its use spreads to those working with them, who seek professional credibility and to become a part of the ingroup. Stewart agrees, saying that "*Ministers feel like imposters*" when joining government departments, the detail of which they might know very little.[27] But he

20 M. Kaldor, "Revolutions of War" on *The Western Way of War,* 8 April 2021. <www.spotify.com>.

21 Coker, *War in an age of risk*: 34.

22 Knight *et al., Hard choices ahead* (Chatham House. London. 2012)*:* 24.

23 Norris, "Military Censorship and the Body Count in the Persian Gulf War": 238 and 230.

24 Laity and Shea interviews.

25 P. Roberts, interview with author, 12 May 2021.

26 Kenneth Waltz, *Foreign Policy and Democratic Politics* (Longmans: London, 1968), 141.

27 R. Seely, interview, March 24, 2021 and Loyn, interview.

also argues this does not remove the responsibility from the communicator (politician) to speak to the audience appropriately, to act as a "*translator*".[28] Sanitised language should not be excused as jargon used in the wrong setting; jargon can be valuable. While jargon may be difficult for outsiders to understand, its intent is to act as a shorthand, or to confer ingroup associations, its intent is neither to expressly remove negative designations nor to communicate with an outgroup.[29] This distinguishes it from sanitised language.

Law and policy also shape how public authorities communicate. There are technical constraints, in some circumstances, on what events or policies can be called and how they can be described. As Chapter 4 detailed, when answering Select Committee questions, Ministers and officials were aware of the dangers of being accused of (illegal) assassination by allowing their language to give the impression of there being a policy of targeted killing. Their responses on regime change in Libya 2011 were similarly shaped by the law. Public authorities are also understandably nervous litigation given their experiences with firms such as Public Interest Lawyers. However, when there is a gap between the apparent reality and the narrative, other, longer term dangers exist, specifically the reduction in trust and understanding of the electorate. The study turns to these impacts shortly.

Further to these explanations, interviewees pointed to the need of senior officials and politicians to retain "wiggle room", the freedom to adapt and change course as circumstances change or to avoid being held to account. This often leads to deliberately opaque language that lacks specificity, allowing the speaker to adapt their position. While this is understandable, at times necessary, and often in the single instance not damaging, there are dangers inherent in this tactic, more of which below.[30] Stewart offers another angle, that some politicians corrupt their thinking through self-deception and this is exposed in their language.[31] In this instance, members of public authorities have convinced themselves of their own, sanitised, narrative to the point that they believe it.[32] This sees them acting as involuntary false witnesses, where they don't know they are giving inaccurate accounts.[33]

28 Stewart, interview.

29 Abrantes, "Euphemism and co-operation in discourse": 87.

30 Interview with Political Advisor, April 2021.

31 Stewart, interview.

32 A. Galeotti, "Liars or self-deceived? Reflections on political deception," in: *Political Studies*, 63 (2015): 887–902.

33 G. Carafilgio, *Involuntary witness* (Bitter Lemon Press: London. 2005).

3 Does This Matter?

Expanding on the arguments made in Chapter 1, the public seem to care about Defence when it is visible, not necessarily when it matters.[34] Defence is routinely low on the list of issues that decide elections, in 2017 and 2019 Defence was tenth; in some senses this reflects a job well done by the military.[35] But between 62% and 69% of the public does worry about their lack of understanding of the military.[36] It appears that popular culture, books, video games, film and images from conflict zones, with all their limitations, "top up" the public intuitive understanding of war.[37] Some question if this is sufficient and if therefore there is no incentive for the public authorities to discuss the harsh side of violence.[38]

However, it is because popular culture appears dominant in the development of public understanding that the quality of the communication between the public authorities, including their use of language, and electorate is important.[39] This is especially the case since Defence is now committed to competing with its adversaries all the time without being at a declared state of war with anyone.[40] This means Defence is likely to conduct operations outside the public consciousness, certainly outside public scrutiny, and beyond the intuitive public understanding of war and violence.

Sir Jeremy Greenstock argues that the deliberate use of sanitised language can be right and proper. The authorities should shield the public from the intricacies of the application of hard power because it is the very role of public service to shoulder the burdens of violence uncomplainingly; this is what the public expects of them.[41] Further to this, Greenstock and senior officers argue that mystique, Kissinger's concept of constructive ambiguity and secrecy are useful tools of diplomacy, negotiation and military operations. Governments do not want to explain exactly what they can, or will, do, as this would cede

34 Sengupta, interview.

35 S. Prescott-Smith, "Which Issues will decide the general election" (YouGov. November 7, 2019) <www.youGov.co.uk>.

36 Royal British Legion, *How much do you know about the Armed Forces?* Last accessed on May 24, 2021, <https://www.britishlegion.org.uk>; Lord Ashcroft, "The Armed Forces & Society: The military in Britain – through the eyes of Service personnel, employers and the public" (May 2012), <www.lordashcroftpolls.com>.

37 Ingham and Roberts, interviews.

38 D. Nicholls, interview with author. May 24, 2021.

39 Roberts interview.

40 Ministry of Defence, *Global Britain in a competitive age.*

41 J. Greenstock, interview with author 21 May 2021.

advantage to adversaries and competitors.[42] Shea also notes the difficulties of working with partners and Allies. For example, NATO must balance the divergent demands of American and German audiences, who have very different views on the value, and necessity, of violence. The competing demands on the message make communicating about violence challenging.[43]

Having looked at why public authorities use sanitised language, the study now examines its potential negative impacts. It affects the electorate's confidence in the public authorities and their understanding of the use of violence. These two core issues create, as Loyn says, a "*democratic deficit*",[44] and reduce the freedoms the public authorities enjoy.

4 Reduced Trust

As discussed in Chapter 2, the foundation of operational freedom enjoyed by the UK's public authorities is trust, probably built on transparency. The use of sanitised language unnecessarily erodes this foundation, paradoxically reducing the freedoms that the public authorities are probably trying to secure through its use. The public is hawkish when it comes to security, 52% support overseas intervention to protect Britons on principle, and nearly 80% support action to protect British territory.[45] Summarising arguments made in Chapter 2, Dandeker says public can tolerate considerable costs, "where the mission is clearly explained and the costs relative to the interests at stake are convincingly demonstrated by the Government to the public".[46] Given the support for hard power, incentives to hide its use seem to be ill-founded.

It appears that the use of sanitised language is an unnecessary short-term tactic that comes at a cost to longer-term issues. Machiavelli's argument that because most people will never find out about it, dishonesty is useful,[47] is not directly transferable to the UK's modern political environment, full of inquiries, where the relationship between the public and the politicians should demonstrate "*the virtues of a friendship between equals*".[48] Here the lack of transparency reinforces public mistrust in Government that in the end undermines the

42 *Ibid.*, and interviews with senior officers.

43 Shea, interview.

44 Loyn, interview.

45 Knight, *Hard choices ahead: 24.*

46 C. Dandeker, personal communications. May 3, 2021.

47 N. Machiavelli, *The Prince,* (Penguin: London. 2004).

48 Stewart, interview.

public authorities' freedom of action. In the UK, there is evidence of rising mistrust in politicians since 2000.[49] Only 37% of voters trust the Prime Minister to tell the truth in a debate over military action,[50] 56% believe politicians are more likely, than in the "past few years" to lie or mislead the public. 73% of the public believe it is wrong to lie, even for reasons of national security.[51] The public value trust and transparency. The Armed Forces on the other hand enjoy considerable public respect.[52] While this may insulate the Armed Forces from negative public opinion, it does not protect the Government and public authorities they serve. It is these authorities that give the Armed Forces their freedoms; when they are constrained so too are the Armed Forces. The erosion of trust affects the Armed Forces, even if indirectly.

5 Lack of Understanding

Sanitised language reduces public understanding of national use of violence, and this creates a "democratic deficit".[53] The electorate cannot be expected to accurately understand the state's use of violence without sufficient accurate information. If public understanding of the use of violence is unlikely to be accurate, their ability to play an effective role in the democratic process is undermined. And as Habermas argues, informed publics are central to a functioning democracy.[54] In this way, through the use of strategic language and attempts to control the narratives of war, public authorities exert power over the electorate.

The public are in a weak democratic position vis-à-vis their knowledge of war as there is insufficient organic understanding of violence in the electorate for a truly effective participatory or representative democracy. This is evidenced by the low number of people in the electorate that have sufficient experience of war to guide their understanding; only five percent of the population over the age of 16 are veterans or serving in the Armed

49 P. Whiteley *et al.*, "Why Do Voters Lose Trust in Governments? Public Perceptions of Government Honesty and Trustworthiness in Britain 2000–2013," in: *British Journal of Politics & International Relations* 18, no. 1 (2016): 234.

50 YouGov. *Report on British attitudes to Defence Security and the Armed Forces,* October 25, 2014, <www.yougov.co.uk>.

51 Edelman, *2020 trust barometer UK results*, <www.edelman.co.uk> last accessed 7 May 2021.

52 C. Dandeker, *et al.* "The UK's Armed Forces: public support for the troops but not their missions." in: *British Social Attitudes Survey 2012*. NatCen, <www.bsa.natcen.ac.uk> 152.

53 Loyn, interview.

54 L. Thomassen, *Habermas: a guide for the perplexed* (Continuum: London. 2010): 11.

Forces.[55] This mirrors the lack of veterans in Parliament. Over time this affects how the public understands, and makes decisions about, the use of violence. As Colley, Shea, Brunk *et al.* note that in the absence of experience the public are unlikely to use specific data to inform decisions on the use of force, but are more likely to use heuristics, narratives and intuition.[56] These decision-making frameworks are an aggregation of multiple sources of understanding. Along with myth, they drive public instincts because they resonate and linger in society longer than individual data points.[57]

In this context the use of sanitised language in the single instance is not damaging, but its persistent use is. Intuition and decision-making frameworks cannot accurately reflect modern conflict, especially when the detail of it is sanitised, because they rely on historical and cultural interpretations of violence. For intuitive understanding to be useful it must not be too far from reality, bastardising what Michael Howard said of military science, " it is the task of [official communication] to prevent [public understanding] from being too badly wrong."[58] Without accurate and clear information being added to the pool from which the public draws its understanding, the gap between reality and perception necessarily widens. This in turn reduces the public's ability to draw relevant conclusions and therefore to meaningfully participate in democratic activity.

This widening of the gap has exacerbated the speed at which the character of conflict is changing; previously relevant conceptions of conflict, upon which intuition is based, are outdated quickly. The character of conflict is changing so rapidly that some question whether the nature of conflict is changing. In particular, violence's increasing use of complex science, such as artificial intelligence or quantum encryption, makes it difficult to understand the detail and the implications of conflict.[59] As even the famous physicist Niels Bohr said "If anybody says he can think about quantum physics without getting giddy, that only shows he has not understood the first thing about them."[60] Further to this, the military now talks of hybrid war, activity below the threshold of war, and the grey zone; these ideas are likely alien to the lay person, and separate from

55 United Kingdom, Ministry of Defence, *Annual Population Survey: UK Armed Forces Veterans residing in Great Britain, 2017* (31 January 2019).

56 See Chapter 2 for fuller consideration of these.

57 Esch, "Legitimising the "War on terror": political Myth in Official level Rhetoric": 386.

58 M. Howard. "Military Science in an Age of Peace," in: *Journal of the Royal United Services Institute*, 119.2, March 1974: 7.

59 C. Coker, *Warrior Geeks* (Hurst: Oxford. 2019): 189.

60 <https://wiseowlquotes.com/niels-bohr/>, last accessed on May 23, 2021.

common conceptions of war and peace.[61] At the heart of these ideas is the need to keep adversaries guessing, using ambiguity as a tool; this is in tension with the commitment to keep the electorate informed. This tension does not appear to be resolved.

Further, proponents of democratic peace theory argue that the lack of understanding of violence removes societal constraints on war and escalation. Norris argues that by removing the true mental images of war, war becomes "permanently acceptable".[62] Specifically addressing how surrogate technology impacts this relationship, Dudziak states that "drones are a technological step that further isolates the American people from military action, undermining checks on … endless wars".[63] One could easily replace *drones* with *sanitised language*: "sanitised language further isolates the British people from military action, undermining checks on endless wars".

6 So What?

The preceding arguments are partly abstract in nature, but this does not reduce their importance. Concerns about the quality of democratic dialogue between government and electorate are concrete and might negatively affect the capabilities the UK needs in order to navigate the emerging geopolitical landscape. Resilience is central to this,[64] Greenstock argues that national resilience would be undermined by opening a debate on the value of hard power with an increasingly less violent public, because the public would undervalue it as an instrument of power.[65] But Strachan and Harris argue the opposite, that "the lack of mature public engagement creates a lack of national resilience."[66] If the UK's adversaries interpret this as a lack of confidence in speaking about the value of violence, they might also detect a lack of confidence in using violence. The Government could be inadvertently emboldening adversaries. The UK also loses influence internationally if partners, Allies, and potential partners view this as a decline in the quality of the UK's democratic dialogue, which hitherto has been a source of soft power. This is because, first partners might

61 Joshi, interview.
62 Norris, "Military Censorship and the Body Count in the Persian Gulf War": 224.
63 J. Mayer, "The Predator War", *The New Yorker,* 26 October 2009. <www.newyorker.com>.
64 Fox, interview.
65 Greenstock, interview.
66 Strachan and Harris, *The Utility of Military Force in Understanding Today's Britain:* 24.

migrate to other poles whose offer is more attractive, and second because the UK can no longer negotiate and cajole from a position of moral strength.[67]

7 What Next?

Having argued that there is deliberate use of sanitised language by public authorities, that it has considerable potential inadvertent negative consequences, and that it does matter, the paper now draws together its tentative conclusions with how this research might be developed.

This paper argues that sanitised language plays a role in the official narrative of war; the evidence shows that its use is selective and follows a pattern, which is to some extent explained and justified. Sadly, this paper cannot make an unequivocal judgement on whether sanitised language forms a part of the tool-box of surrogacy, tools that break the socio-political bond between Government and electorate. While there has been valuable contribution from many, some key departments, such as Government communications offices, did not provide comment at this busy time. To make good these gaps, further research is needed. First, a representative survey of the public's understanding of war, its language and depiction is needed, providing clusters of understanding around certain commonly used terms. It could be supported by evidence for public interest in, and tolerance of, state violence; the UK could emulate the French Government's testing of public acceptance of high casualties through focus groups on Exercise Orion, hypothetical war with Russia.[68] Second, more detailed primary research is needed with the key departments and individuals in the public authorities; without their input, the study is vulnerable to challenge that it neglects their perspective.

Further, the fact that arguments in defence of sanitised language tend to be practical and arguments for "the prosecution" begin with the moral, or philosophical (but end up as practical) complicates this paper's judgements, which must weigh the practical against the philosophical. But the issues above do not mean the paper cannot offer tentative conclusions and highlight concerns. After all, this is why *critical* discourse analysis was chosen as the tool of the study; the paper is written in the spirit of productive iconoclasm not hard revolution.

67 Stewart, interview.
68 Coker, personal communications.

The paper argues that sanitised language is evident where the hallmarks surrogacy are apparent. The use of those other tools of surrogacy, drones, special forces, and proxies is deliberate. On balance, this correlation seems significant, and worthy of further investigation. However, while this may dilute the socio-political ties, and increase the power of the public authorities relative to the electorate, the public authorities are unlikely to be seeking to break this bond, upon which they appear (doctrinally at least) to rely for support and/or re-election.

Though there may be no deliberate effort to break or dilute the socio-political ties, and there may be short term advantages to this use of surrogacy, evidence suggests there are negative consequences to its persistent use. These consequences affect the quality of the democracy in the UK, and the freedoms that public authorities enjoy. If the authorities avoid discussion about the value of hard power, they are in danger of inoculating the public to its value, and in so doing undermining the visible quality of the UK's democracy, its soft power. Any growth of these consequences must be arrested. The public authorities would likely challenge that it is naïve to come to the conclusions of the study without all the detail of their circumstances. But, at apparently little political cost, and with potential benefits, the public authorities could be clearer in their communication about violence. Though Simpson may be stretching the case by musing "there is no incentive to use" unclear language, he certainly flags that the balance is wrong.[69] Addressing this balance could well lead to a more effective explanation of the value, and therefore public acceptance, of hard power, the threat or use of violence as an instrument of the state.

69 E. Simpson, interview with author, April 7, 2021.

Bibliography

ABC, "ADF Chief Angus Campbell offers apology in wake of Afghanistan war crimes report," 19 November 2020, accessed at <https://www.abc.net.au/news/2020-11-19/defence-chief-angus-campbell-afghanistan-apology-transcript/12899854>.

ABC, "Australian planes involved in Iraqi airstrike which killed civilians," 31 January 2019. Last accessed <https://www.abc.net.au/news/2019-02-01/iraqi-civilians-killed-in-airstrike-australia-involved-in/10766770>.

Abrantes, A. "Euphemism and co-operation in discourse" in Grillo (ed.), *Power and domination: dialogism and the empowering property of communication* (John Benjamins: Amsterdam: 2005): 85–102.

Agricultural Extension in South Asia. *Blog 132-Research onion: A systematic Approach to Designing Research methodology.* Last accessed on May 25, 2021 through <https://www.aesanetwork.org/research-onion-a-systematic-approach-to-designing-research-methodology/>.

Al Jazeera. Editorial *guidelines*. Last accessed May 21, 2021 through <http://www.allied-media.com/aljazeera/Aljazeera_Network_Editorial_Policy_and_Guidelines_for_Advertisements.html>.

All Party Parliamentary Group on Drones, "The UK's Use of Armed Drones: working with partners," published at <www.appadrones.org.uk>, 2018 (accessed on 1 March 2021).

Allen, A. and Goddard, R. "The domestication of Foucault: Government, critique, war" in: *History of Human Sciences* 27(2) (2014): 26–53.

Ashcroft, L. "The Armed Forces & Society: The military in Britain – through the eyes of Service personnel, employers and the public", May 2012, accessed through <https://lordashcroftpolls.com/wp-content/uploads/2012/05/THE-ARMED-FORCES-SOCIETY.pdf>.

Associated Press, "Mosul is a graveyard: final IS battle kills 9000 civilians," 21 December, 2017. Last accessed 25 May 2021 through <https://apnews.com/article/bbea7094fb954838a2fdc11278d65460>.

Balzacq, T. "The Three faces of Securitisation: political agency, audience and content," in: *European Journal of International relations* 11(2), 2005: 171–201.

Barko, L. "Editorial policies and news discourse – how Al Jazeera's implicit guidelines shape its coverage of Middle East conflicts," in: *Journalism* 00(0), 2019: 1–18.

Barry, J. "The day we stopped the war," in: *Newsweek*, January 1, 1992. Accessed through <https://www.newsweek.com/day-we-stopped-war-197642>.

Bassford, C. and Villacres, E. "Reclaiming the Clausewitzian Trinity" in: *Parameters* Autumn (1995): 9–19.

Bassford, C., "The primacy of Policy and the 'Trinity' in Clausewitz's mature thought" in: Strachan, H, Herberg-Rothe, A, *Clausewitz in the Twenty-First Century*, (Oxford: Oxford University Press, 2007).

Baurillard, J. *The Gulf War did not take place*, (Indiana University Press: Indiana, 1991).

Beale, J. "Islamic State: US military says RAF airstrikes may have killed civilians," *Thew BBC*. 16 March 2020. Accessed at <https://www.bbc.co.uk/news/uk-51900898>.

Beck, U. "The Silence of Words: On Terror and War," in: *Security Dialogue* 34(3): 255–267.

Boone, J. "Battle of Babaji: A fight for hearts and minds in Afghanistan, but none are to be found." *The Guardian*, June 24, 2009. Accessed through <https://www.theguardian.com/uk/2009/jun/24/british-soldiers-taliban-afghanistan>.

Bottici, C. and Challand, B. "Rethinking Political Myth: The Clash of Civilisations as a self-fulfilling prophecy" in: *European Journal of Social Theory* 9(3): 315–336.

Bousquet, A. *The Scientific Way of Warfare: Order and Chaos on the Battlefields of Modernity*, (Hurst & Co: London, 2009).

Braun, M., and Brunstetter, D. "Rethinking the Criterion for Assessing Cia-targeted Killings: Drones, Proportionality and Jus Ad Vim," in: *Journal of Military Ethics* 12, no. 4 (2013): 304–24.

Brewer, P., K. Gross, S. Aday, and L. Willnat. "International Trust and Public Opinion About World Affairs," in: *American Journal of Political Science* 48, no. 1 (2004): 993–109.

Brewis, J. "The ethics of researching friends: on convenience sampling in qualitative management and organisation studies," in: *British Journal of Management*. 25 (2014): 849–862.

Brown, C. "Straw admits failure to record civilian deaths is 'odd'." *The Independent*. May 19, 2004. Accessed through <https://search.proquest.com/docview/310622390/4F98FD4760474366PQ/7?accountid=11862>.

Brunk, G., Secrest, D., and Tamashiro, H., "The Underlying Structure of Ethical Beliefs toward War" in: *Journal of Peace Research*, 26.2 (1989): 139–152.

Brunk, G. Secrest, D., and Tamashiro, H., *Understanding Attitudes about War*, (Pittsburgh: University of Pittsburgh Press, 1996).

Burridge, K. *Is political correctness a euphemism for euphemism?* (1999), <www. abc.net>, last accessed 7 May 2021. <https://www.abc.net.au/radionational/programs/archived/linguafranca/is-political-correctness-a-euphemism-for-euphemism/3567154>.

Burton, J. "The culture of apathy and dishonesty within the British Army", in *The Wavell Room*. December 9, 2020. Accessed through <https://wavellroom.com/2020/12/09/cultural-apathy-and-dishonesty-within-the-british-army-say-do-gap/?fbclid=IwAR0VUm00K0ERuO0-UodH7w2zGSBHzW2y01K0FlTBfsu-3cJmYPfdmd9M4Qw#easy-footnote-bottom-1-25384>.

Carafilgio, G. *Involuntary witness* (Bitter Lemon Press: London. 2005).

Carrell, S. and McSmith, A. "UK troops investigated over deaths of 10 civilians; first official recognition of abuse scandal in Minister's report 'slipped out' before recess," in: *Independent on Sunday*. May 30, 2004, <https://search.proquest.com/docview/336920267/4F98FD4760474366PQ/66?accountid=11862>.

Carson, A. *Secret Wars: Covert Conflict in International Politics* (Princeton University Press: Princeton, 2018).

Chilcot, J., "The Report of the Iraq Inquiry", UK: House of Commons, <https/lassets.publishing.service.gov.uk/government/uploads/system/uploadslattachment da ta/file/535407/The Report of the Iraq Inquiry – Executive Summary.pdf> (Accessed 21 February, 2021).

Clarke, Bruce, International Security Editor at *The Economist*, interview with author 3 June 2021.

Clausewitz, C. Von, Howard, M., Paret, P., and Reid, B. *On War*, (Princeton: Princeton University Press, 1984).

CNN. "UK: Shot Brazilian's visa expired," July 28, 2005. Accessed through <https://edition.cnn.com/2005/WORLD/europe/07/28/menezes.brazil/index.html>.

Coe, K. "Television News, Public Opinion, and the Iraq War: Do Wartime Rationales Matter?" in: *Communication Research* 40, no. 4 (2013): 486–505.

Coker, C. *Rebooting Clausewitz: "On War" in the twenty-first century*. (New York: Oxford University Press, 2017).

Coker, C. *War in an age of risk* (Polity: Cambridge. 2009).

Coker, C. *Warrior Geeks* (Hurst&Co: Oxford. 2019).

Coker, Professor Christopher, Director LSE IDEAS, interview with author 14 April 2021.

Cole, C. "Flawed questions undermine new UK drone poll data" *Dronewars*. March 26, 2013. Accessed through <https://dronewars.net/2013/03/26/flawed-questions-undermine-new-uk-drone-poll-data/>.

Colley, Dr Tom, Senior Lecturer Department of War Studies KCL, interview with author 14 April 2021.

Colley, T. "Is Britain a force for good? Investigating British citizens' narrative understanding of war," in: *Defence Studies* 17.1 (2017): 1–22.

Colley, T. "What's in it for us? Responses to the UK's strategic narrative on intervention in Libya," in: *The RUSI Journal* 160.4 (2015): 60–69.

Colley, T. "What's in it for us? Responses to the UK's strategic narrative on intervention in Libya," in: *The RUSI Journal* 160.4 (2015): 60–69.

Cook, G. "Discourse analysis" in Simpson, J. (ed.) "Critical Discourse Analysis," in: *The Routledge Handbook of Applied Linguistics*, (Routledge: London, 2011, 431–444).

Cortright, D. and Fairhurst, R. "Assessing the debate on drone warfare," in: D. Cortright, R. Fairhurst, and K. Wall, *Drones and the future of armed conflict* (University of Chicago Press: Chicago, 2015).

Cortright, D., Fairhurst, R., and Wall, K. *Drones and the future of armed conflict* (Chicago University Press: Chicago, 2015).

Cox, R. "Social Forces, States and World Orders: Beyond International Relations Theory," in: *Millennium: Journal of International Studies*. 10.2 (1981): 126–155.

Dahlgreen, W. "Support for Syria airstrikes falls again." YouGov. December 5, 2016. Accessed through <https://yougov.co.uk/topics/politics/articles-reports/2015/12/06/support-syria-air-strikes-falls-again>.

Dahlgreen, W., "ISIS: How 57% came to favour air strikes," YouGov (26 September 2014), accessed at <yougov.co.uk>, last accessed 5 May 2021.

Dandeker, C. *et al.* "Are the Armed Forces Understood and Supported by the Public? A view from the United Kingdom." In *Armed Forces and Society* 41(4), 2015: 688--713.

Dandeker, C. *et al.* "The UK's Armed Forces: public support for the troops but not their missions." in *British Social Attitudes Survey 2012*. NatCen. <www.bsa.natcen.ac.uk>, last accessed 7 May 2021. (138–155).

Dandeker, C., "The military in democratic societies" in: *Society*. 38.6. 2001: 16–24.

Dandeker, Professor Christopher, Professor of Military Sociology KCL, personal communications 19 April 2021.

Darley, W. "War Policy, Public Support, and the Media," in: *Parameters* 35, no. 2 (2005): 121–134.

Dearden, L. "UK government 'has blood on its hands' over Yemen conflict but poll shows 42% of British public do not know war exists," in: *The Independent* October 28, 2018. Accessed through <https://www.independent.co.uk/news/uk/home-news/yemen-war-saudi-arabia-bombing-british-uk-arms-exports-public-poll-keith-vaz-blood-hands-a8604521.html> www.dictionary.cambridge.org/dictionary/english/annihilate.

Dearden, L. "UK government does not know how many civilians killed in Syria and Iraq airstrikes, minister admits," in: *The Independent*. April 2, 2019. Accessed through <https://www.independent.co.uk/news/world/middle-east/isis-syria-air strikes-civilians-killed-casualties-iraq-uk-raf-a8851476.html>.

Drake, L. and Donohue, W. "Communicative Framing Theory in Conflict Resolution" in: *Communication Research* 23.3. June 1996: 297–322.

Dunne, T. Kurki, M. and Smith, S. (eds.) *International relations theory; disciplines and diversity* (Oxford University Press: Oxford, 2016).

Edelman. *2020 trust barometer UK results*, <www.edelman.co.uk>, last accessed 7 May 2021.

Fairclough, I. and Fairclough, N. *Political Discourse Analysis: A method for advanced students* (Routledge: Abingdon, 2012).

Fairhurst, G. and Uhi-Bien, M. "Organisational discourse analysis (ODA): examining leadership as a rational process," in: *Leadership Quarterly* 23. 2012: 1043–1062.

Fan, W. and Yan, Z. "Factors affecting response rates of the web survey: a systematic review" in: *Computers in Human Behaviour* 26 (2010): 132–139.

Farndale, E. "High Commitment Performance Management: the roles of justice and trust," in: *Personnel Review* 40.1 (2010): 5–23.

Financial times. *Boris Johnson benefits from UK voters' lack of trust in politicians*. <www.ft.com> last accessed 21 January 2021.

Flick, U. *An introduction to qualitative research,* (Sage: UK, 2018).

Forster, A. *Armed Forces and Society in Europe* (Basingstoke: Palgrave Macmillan, 2006).

Foucault, M. *Security, Territory, Population: Lectures at the College de France, 1977* (Palgrave Macmillan: London, 2007).

Fox, Robert, Defence Editor at *The Evening Standard,* interview with author, 14 May 2021.

Frankfurt, H. *On Bullshit* (Princeton University Press: Princeton. 2009).

Freedman, L. (ed.) *War* (Oxford University Press: Oxford, 1994).

Fussell, P. (ed.), *The Bloody Game: An Anthology of Modern War* (Scribners: London, 1991).

Galeotti, A. "Liars or self-deceived? Reflections on political deception," in *Political Studies*. 63 (2015): 887–902.

Galeotti, A. "Liars or self-deceived? Reflections on political self-deception," in *Political Studies.* 63 (2015): 887–902.

Glees, A., Davies, P., and Morrison, I. *The Open Side of Secrecy* (The Social Affairs Unit: London, 2006).

Gray, J. "Steven Pinker is wrong about violence and war," *The Guardian,* May 13, 2015 accessed through <https://www.theguardian.com/books/2015/mar/13/john-gray-steven-pinker-wrong-violence-war-declining>.

Greenstock, J. *Iraq, the cost of war* (Heinemann: London, 2016).

Greenstock, Sir Jeremy, Former UK's Permanent Representative to United Nations and UK Special representative for Iraq, interview with author 21 May 2021.

Grimmelikhuijsen, S., G. Porumbescu, B. Hong, and T. Im, "The Effect of Transparency on Trust in Government: A Cross-National Comparative Experiment," in: *Public Administration Review* 73, no. 4 (2013): 575–86.

Guillaume, X. "How to do things with silence: rethinking the centrality of speech to the securitization framework" in: *Security Dialogue* Vol 49 No 6, 2018: 476–492.

Haddock, E. *On Words: Clausewitz, Bin Laden, and Public Support* (Washington: National War College, 2002).

Harris, R. and Strachan, H. *The Utility of Military Force and Public Understanding in Today's Britain* (RAND Europe. 2020).

Hasian, M., *Drones Warfare and Lawfare in a Post-Heroic age* (University of Alabama Press: Alabama, 2016).

Hetherington, M., and Globetti, S. "Political Trust and Racial Policy Preferences," *American Journal of Political Science* 46, no. 2 (2002): 253–275.

Heuser, B. *Reading Clausewitz* (London: Pimlico, 2002).

Higate, P. and Cameron, A. "Reflectivity and researching the military" in: *Armed Forces and Society* 32.2 (2006): 219-233.

HM Government Press release, "PM to announce largest military investment in 30 years" (2020). <https://www.gov.uk/government/news/pm-to-announce-largest-military-investment-in-30-years> last accessed on 1 March 2021.

HM Government Press Release. "2010 to 2015 government policy: armed forces covenant" <https://www.gov.uk/government/publications/2010-to-2015-government-policy-armed-forces-covenant/2010-to-2015-government-policy-armed-forces-covenant>, last accessed 10 February 2021.

Hook, G. "Making Nuclear Weapons Easier to Live With: The Political Role of Language in Nuclearization," in *Security Dialogue: Bulletin of Peace Proposals*. 16(1): 67–77.

Hopkins, N. "An unnecessary death: commander speaks out over 'blue on blue' shooting," in: *The Guardian,* March 14, 2014. Accessed through <https://www.theguardian.com/uk-news/2014/mar/14/british-soldier-blue-on-blue-killing>.

Hopkins, N. "Libya: NATO admits civilian deaths in Tripoli air raid," *The Guardian*, June 20, 2011 accessed through <https://www.theguardian.com/world/2011/jun/19/nato-libya-strike-civilian-deaths>.

Howard, M. "Military Science in an Age of Peace," in *Journal of the Royal United Services Institute*. 119.2. (March 1974): 3–11.

Hughes, G. "Syria and the Perils of Proxy Warfare," in: *Small Wars & Insurgencies* 25, no. 3 (2014): 522–38.

Hughes, G. "War in the Grey Zone: Historical Reflections and Contemporary Implications," in *Survival* 62, no. 3 (2020): 131–58.

Human Rights Watch. *Needless deaths in the Gulf War* (New York, 1991).

Ingham, Dr Sarah, author of *The Military Covenant,* interview with author, 27 April 2021.

Jones, S. "Reluctance to use force is 'encouraging' grave threat: Defence speech," in: *The Financial Times*, September 16, 2015. Accessed through <https://search.proquest.com/docview/1722533014/AAB9CF8F6ED94025PQ/16?accountid=11862>.

Joshi, Shashank, Defence editor at *The Economist,* interview with author on 21 April 2021.

Kaldor, M., "Revolutions of War" on *The Western Way of War podcast.* 8 April 2021. <www.spotify.com>, last accessed 7 May 2021.

Kasher, A. "Public Trust in a Military Force" in: *Journal of Military Ethics* 2, no. 1. (2003): 20–45.

Kasher, A., "Public Trust in a Military Force" in *Journal of Military Ethics* 2, no. 1. (2003).

Kellner, P. "Syria, but do help Obama." YouGov. September 1, 2013. Accessed through <https://yougov.co.uk/topics/politics/articles-reports/2013/09/01/voters-tell-cameron-dont-bomb-syria-do-help-obama>.

Kemp, R. "In modern war civilian deaths are inevitable: NATO's mistake in Libya is tragic, but our distaste for such casualties plays into Gaddafi's hands," in: *The Times,* June 21, 2011. Accessed through <https://search.proquest.com/docview/872754545/4F98FD4760474366PQ/63?accountid=11862>.

King, K. "Policing Language: Linguistic security and the sources of ethnic conflict. A Rejoinder" in: *Security Dialogue*. Vol 28 no. 4. 1997: 493–496.

Knight, J., Niblett, R., and Raines, T. *Hard Choices Ahead* (Chatham House: London, 2012), accessed through <https://d25d2506sfb94s.cloudfront.net/cumulus_uploads/document/pborllro2g/07.2012%20Chatham%20House%20-%20%27British%20attitudes%20towards%20the%20UK%27s%20international%20priorities%27%2C%202012.pdf>.

Knight, M. "Getting Past the Impasse: Framing as A Tool for Public Relations," in: *Public Relations Review*. 25(3): 381–398.

Krieg, A. and Rickli, J.-M., "Surrogate warfare: the art of war in the 21 Century?" in: *Defence Studies*. 18, no. 2. (2018): 113–130.

Krieg, A. "Beyond the Trinitarian institutionalization of the Warrior Ethos – A Normative Conceptualization of Soldier and Contractor Commitment in Post-Modern Conflict," in: *Defence Studies* 14, no. 1 (2014): 56–75.

Krieg, A. "Externalizing the Burden of War: The Obama Doctrine and US Foreign Policy in the Middle East," in: *International Affairs* 92, no. 1 (2016): 97–113.

Laity, Dr Mark, former NATO spokesperson, interview with author 8 April 2021.

Laity, M. *Twitter*, March 19 2021; last accessed 8 April 2021.

Lakoff, G. *Metaphor and War: The Metaphor System Used to Justify War in the Gulf*, (University of California, Draft, 1991).

Lamb, Christina, journalist and author, interview with author 29 May 2021.

Lee, P. *Rights, Wrongs and Drones: Warfare, Ethics and the Challenge of Just War reasoning*. 2013.

Lee, P. *Truth Wars. The Politics of Climate Change, Military Intervention and Financial Crisis*, (Palgrave Macmillan: London. 2015).

Lewis, J. and Nicholls, C. "Design Issues", in: J. Ritchie (ed.) *Qualitative research practise: a guide for social science students and researchers*, (SAGE: Los Angeles, 2014: 47–76).

Lonsdale, D. *The Nature of War in the Information Age: Clausewitzian Future*, (London: Frank Cass, 2004).

Lord Ashcroft, *The Armed Forces and Society*; May 2012 accessed through <https://lordashcroftpolls.com/wp-content/uploads/2012/05/THE-ARMED-FORCES-SOCIETY.pdf>.

Loyn, David, journalist and author, interview, interview with author 3 May 2021.

Maartens, B. "From Propaganda to 'Information': Reforming Government Communications in Britain." In: *Contemporary British History* 30:4 (2016): 542–562.

Machiavelli, N. *The Prince*, (Penguin: London. 2004).

Mahnken, T. "Strategic Theory" in Baylis, J., Cohen, E., Gray, C., Wirtz, (eds.) *Strategy in the contemporary world*, (2nd ed. Oxford: Oxford University Press, 2007).

Margolis, M. and Mauser, G. "Public opinion as a Dependent Variable: A Framework for analysis," in: *Political Communication*. 6:2 (1989) 87–108.

Marsh, D. and Furlong, P. "A skin not a sweater: ontology and epistemology in political science," in: V. Lowndes, D. Marsh and G. Stoker. *Theory and methods in political science*, (Palgrave MacMillan: New York, 2008): 18–410.

Mayer, J. "The Predator War", *The New Yorker*, 26 October 2009. Accessed through <https://www.newyorker.com/magazine/2009/10/26/the-predator-war>.

McLay, Michael, interview with author 21 May 2021.

Michaels, J. and Ford, M. "Bandwagonistas: rhetorical re-description, strategic choice and politics of counter insurgency," in: *Small Wars and Insurgencies*. 22;02, 2011: 352–384.

Michaels, J. *The Discourse trap* (Palgrave Macmillan: New York, 2013).

Military Officers' Association of America. "Colin Powell remembers Desert Strom 25 years later". December 23, 2015. Accessed through <https://www.moaa.org/content/publications-and-media/features-and-columns/moaa-features/Colin-Powell-Remembers-Desert-Storm-25-years-later/>.

Ministry of Defence, *The Armed Forces Covenant*. 2000.

Mueller, J. *War, Presidents and Public Opinion* (John Wiley: New York, 1973).

Mueller, J. *War, Presidents and Public Opinion* (New York: John Wiley & Sons. 1973).

Neisser, P. "Targets" in Collins., J. and Glover, R. (eds.) *Collateral Language* (New York University Press: New York, 2002).

Neumann, I. "Discourse Analysis" in A. Klotz and D. Prakash (eds.) *Qualitative Methods in International Relations* (Palgrave MacMillan: New York, 2008: 61–77).

Nicholls, Dominic, Defence Editor at *The Telegraph*, interview with author 24 May 2021.

Norris, M. "Military Censorship and the Body Count in the Persian Gulf war," in *cultural Critique* 19. Autumn, 1991: 223–245.

O' Halloran, K. "Critical Discourse Analysis," in: J. Simpson (ed.) *The Routledge Handbook of Applied Linguistics* (Routledge: Abingdon, 2011): 445–65.

O'Driscoll, C. "Fear and Trust: the shooting of Jean Charles de Menezes and the War on Terror," in: *Millennium: Journal of International Studies* 36.2. 2008: 149–170.

O'Driscoll, C. "Talking about Just War: Obama in Oslo, Bush at War." In *Politics*. 31(2), 2011: 82–90.

Ormston, R. *et al.* "The foundations of qualitative research." In J. Ritchie (ed.) *Qualitative research practise: a guide for social science students and researchers* (SAGE: Los Angeles. 2014: 1–25).

Parker, Dr Glen, interview with author 26 April 2021.

Parris, M., "In the fog, remember: victory is impossible in Afghanistan," *The Times* 4 July 2009.

Pars, M., "Six Strategy Lessons from Clausewitz and Sun Tzu," in: *Journal of Public Affairs* 13, no. 3 (2013): 329–34.

Patrikarakos, D. *War in 140 Characters* (New York: Hachette. 2017).

Payne, K. "The Media as an Instrument of War," in: *Parameters*. Spring, 2005: 81–93.

Peel, Quentin, interview with author on 4 May 2021.

Pick, Hella, interview with author 20 April 2021.

Political Advisor, interview with author 2 April 2021.

Poole, S. *Unspeak* (Abacus: London, 2007).

Popkin, S. *et al.* (eds.) *Elements of Reason: cognition, choice and the bounds of rationality* (Cambridge University Press: Cambridge, 2000).

Prescott-Smith, S. "Which issues will decide the general election?" YouGov <https://yougov.co.uk/topics/politics/articles-reports/2019/11/07/which-issues-will-decide-general-election> last accessed March, 2021.

Rauta, V. "Delegation in distress: an ever-growing semantic field?" in: Rauta, A. *et al.* "A Symposium – debating 'surrogate warfare' and the transformation of war" in: *Defence Studies* 19, no. 4 (2019); 410–430.

Reicher, S. "Transparency is Key in a Crisis – so why isn't the British Government being straight with us?" *The Guardian*, May 13, 2020.

Rickland, C. "Iran's surrogate warfare and the future of the concept" in Rauta, A. *et al.* "A Symposium – debating 'surrogate warfare' and the transformation of war" in: *Defence Studies* 19, no. 4 (2019): 410–430.

Riwi. *Peace Perceptions Poll 2018.* Accessed through <https://www.international-alert.org/sites/default/files/Organisation_PeacePerceptionsPoll_Ed2_EN_2018.pdf>.

Roberts, Dr Peter, Director of Military Science at RUSI, interview with author on 13 May 2021.

Rottinghaus, B. "Presidential leadership on Foreign Policy, Opinion, Polling and the Possible Limits of "crafted talk,"" in *Political Communication* 25:2, 2008: 138–157.

Royal British Legion, "How much do you know about the Armed Forces," last accessed on May 24, 2021 through <https://www.britishlegion.org.uk/stories/how-much-do-you-know-about-the-armed-forces>.

Royal British Legion. "How much do you know about the Armed Forces?" Last accessed on May 18 2021, through <https://www.britishlegion.org.uk/stories/how-much-do-you-know-about-the-armed-forces>.

Salter, M. and Mutlu, C. *Research Methods in Critical Security Studies: an introduction* (Routledge: New York, 2012).

Saunders, M. Lewis, P. and Thornhill, A. *Research Methods for Business Students* (Pearson: Harlow, 2019).

Scharrer, E. and Blackburn, G. "Images of Injury: Graphic News Visuals' Effects on Attitudes toward the Use of Unmanned Drones" in: *Mass Communication and Society* 18 (2015): 799–820.

Seaton, J. *Carnage and the Media* (Allen Lane: London. 2005): xx.

Seely, Robert, interview with author 24 March 2021.

Sengupta, Kim, Defence and Security Editor at *The* Guardian, interview with author 10 May 2021.

Senior Officer 1, interview with author 10 May 2021.

Senior Officer 2, interview with author 19 May 2021.

Senior Officer 3, interview with author 1 June 2021.

Senior Officer 4, interview with author 3 June 2021.

Settle, M. "Pressure grows for Iraq war as Brown avoids issue: failure to count civilian deaths labelled 'grotesque'" in: *The Herald.* December 19, 2008. Accessed through <https://search.proquest.com/docview/333146300/4F98FD4760474366PQ/26?accountid=11862>.

Shaw, M. *The New Western Way of War: Risk Transfer War and Its Crisis in Iraq* (Cambridge: Polity, 2005).

Shea, Professor Jamie, former NATO spokesperson, interview with author 7 April 2021.

Simpson, E. *War from the Ground up: Twenty-first Century Combat as Politics. Crises in World Politics* (London: Hurst, 2012).

Simpson, Emile, interview with author 7 April 2021.

Smith, E. "Don't be beguiled by Orwell: using plain and clear language is not always a moral virtue" in: *Newstatesman*, February 9, 2013.

Smith, M. "Are the troops heroes? Americans, Germans and Britons feel very differently." YouGov. September 26, 2018. Accessed through <https://yougov.co.uk/topics/politics/articles-reports/2018/09/26/are-troops-heroes-americans-britons-and-germans-fe>.

Smith, M. "Jeremy Corbyn is on the right side of public opinion about foreign policy: except for the Falklands." YouGov. May 30, 2017 accessed through <www.yougov.com> <https://yougov.co.uk/topics/politics/articles-reports/2017/05/30/jeremy-corbyn-right-side-public-opinion-foreign-po>.

Smith, M. "Jeremy Corbyn is on the right side of public opinion on foreign policy: except for the Falklands." YouGov. May 30, 2017. Accessed through <https://yougov.co.uk/topics/politics/articles-reports/2017/05/30/jeremy-corbyn-right-side-public-opinion-foreign-po>.

Sommervile, Q. "Afghanistan's 'green on blue' collapse of trust," The BBC October 7, 2012. Accessed through <https://www.bbc.co.uk/news/world-south-asia-19834021>.

Stacey, K and Warrell, H., "Civilian deaths pile on pressure on Libya Campaign," *The Financial Times*, June 20, 2011. Accessed through <https://search.proquest.com/docview/872863599/4F98FD4760474366PQ/8?accountid=11862>.

Steele, Jonathan, interview with author 3 May 2021.

Stewart, Rory, former Secretary of State and deputy Governor in Maysan and Dhi Qar, Iraq, interview with author 26 May 2021.

Strachan, H., Herberg-Rothe, A., *Clausewitz in the Twenty-First Century*, (Oxford: Oxford University Press, 2007).

Strachan, H. "Sir Michael Howard lectures" (online), 18 November 2020.

Strachan, H. *Making strategy work: civil-military relations in Britain and the United States*, (Cambridge: Cambridge University Press, 2013).

The Atlantic, "Counting the dead in Mosul: the civilian death toll in the fight against ISIS is far higher than official estimates," 5 April 2018. Accessed through <https://www.theatlantic.com/international/archive/2018/04/counting-the-dead-in-mosul/556466/>.

The BBC editorial guidelines. Last accessed 24 May 2021 through <https://www.bbc.com/editorialguidelines/guidelines/harm-and-offence/guidelines section 11>.

The BBC, "In quotes: House of Commons debate on Libya action," 22 March 2011, accessed through <https://www.bbc.co.uk/news/uk-politics-12809496>.

The BBC, "Islamic State conflict: UK 'would repeat Syria drone strike,'" last accessed through <www.bbc.co.uk/news/uk-34181475>.

The BBC. *Editorial guidelines,* last accessed May 21, 2021 through <https://www.bbc.co.uk/editorialguidelines/guidelines/war-terror-emergencies>.

The Express, "Britain joins fight to smash ISIS stronghold" October 17, 2016. Accessed through <https://www.express.co.uk/news/world/722197/Britain-fight-Mosul-IS-ISIS-stronghold-Mosul-attack-Michael-Fallon>.

The Glasgow Sunday Herald, "There must be no fog of war over civilian deaths," January 10, 2016.

The Guardian, "David Cameron's Libya War: why the PM felt Gaddafi had to be stopped," 2 October 2011 accessed through <https://www.theguardian.com/politics/2011/oct/02/david-cameron-libyan-war-analysis>.

The Guardian, "Fox Reveals £260m cost of Libya Campaign," 24 June 2011 accessed through <https://www.theguardian.com/politics/2011/jun/23/libya-campaign-has-cost-uk-260m>.

The Guardian, "Police defend Menezes shooting tactics," March 8, 2006. Accessed through <https://www.theguardian.com/uk/2006/mar/08/menezes>.

The Guardian, "US airstrikes target Islamic State militants in Libya," (19 February, 2016) last accessed. <https://www.theguardian.com/world/2016/feb/19/us-airstrikes-target-islamic-state-militants-in-libya>.

The Independent, "RAF airstrike against ISIS fighters in Syria unintentionally killed a civilian says Gavin Williamson," 2 May 2018. Accessed through <https://www.independent.co.uk/news/uk/politics/uk-airstrike-syria-raf-civilian-killed-isis-gavin-williamson-mod-ministry-defence-a8332656.html>.

The Independent, "UK claims it has killed just one civilian in 1700 bombing raids on Iraq and Syria," 7 March 2019, accessed through <https://www.independent.co.uk/news/world/middle-east/syria-iraq-uk-airstrikes-civilian-deaths-raqqa-mod-a8811781.html>.

The New York Times, "Scores of unintended casualties in NATO war in Libya" (18 December, 2011), last accessed on <https://www.nytimes.com/2011/12/18/world/africa/scores-of-unintended-casualties-in-nato-war-in-libya.html>.

The Sunday Herald, "UK drone strikes: MOD document admits terrorists are killed outside conflict zones" (4 February 2018), accessed through <https://www.heraldscotland.com/news/15918600.drones-used-kill-terror-suspects-outside-warzones-bombshell-mod-document-states/>.

Thomas, D., "Security in the balance: How Britain tried to keep its Iraq War secrets," in: *Security Dialogue* 51, No 1 (2019): 77–95.

Thomassen, L. *Habermas: a guide for the perplexed* (Continuum: London. 2010).

Tidy, J. "War Craft: the embodied politics of making war" in *Security Dialogue* 50, No 3, 2019: 220–238.

Time, "A US Commander's year on the Front Line against ISIS in Iraq and Syria," 7 September, 2017. <https://time.com/4931037/lieut-general-stephen-townsend-interview/>.

Time, "Defence Chief James Mattis says the US is bow using 'annihilation tactics' against ISIS" (May 29, 2017), <https://time.com/4797075/james-mattis-islamic-state-annihilation/>.

United Kingdom House of Commons debate. *Liberation of Mosul.* October 18, 2016. Accessed through <https://www.theyworkforyou.com/debates/?id=2016-10-18d.674.2>.

United Kingdom, "Hansard Houses of Commons Debate" (2 December 2015): Column 332. <www.hansard.parliament.uk>.

United Kingdom, "Hansard Houses of Commons Debate," 21 March 2011: Column 707.

United Kingdom, "House of Commons Defence Select Committee – Minutes of Evidence HC 950," accessed through <https://publications.parliament.uk/pa/cm201012/cmselect/cmdfence/950/11042701.htm>.

United Kingdom, "House of Commons Defence Select Committee Ninth Report-Operations in Libya" (25 January 2012), <https://publications.parliament.uk/pa/cm201012/cmselect/cmdfence/950/95005.htm#a10>.

United Kingdom, "House of Lords, House of Commons, Joint Committee on Human Rights. The Government's policy on the use of drones for targeted killing," House of Lords. April 2016. Accessed through <https://publications.parliament.uk/pa/jt201516/jtselect/jtrights/574/574.pdf>.

United Kingdom, "Houses of Parliament debate Hansard," vol. 23. May 4, 1982 accessed through <https://api.parliament.uk/historic-hansard/commons/1982/may/04/falkland-islands-2>.

United Kingdom, "Oral evidence for House of Commons Defence Select Committee Report: UK Military Operations in Syria and Iraq," 26 May 2016, accessed through <www.publication.parliament.uk>.

United Kingdom, "Oral evidence for House of Commons Foreign Affairs Select Committee report: Libya: Examination of intervention and collapse and the UK's future policy options," December 1, 2015, accessed through <http://data.parliament.uk/writtenevidence/committeeevidence.svc/evidencedocument/foreign-affairs-committee/libya-examination-of-intervention-and-collapse-and-the-uks-future-policy-options/oral/25384.html>.

United Kingdom, "Oral evidence for Joint Committee on Human Rights: The Government's policy on the use of drones for targeted killing," 16 December 2015. <www.publications.parliament.uk>.

United Kingdom, "Written evidence for House of Commons Defence Select Committee Report: UK Military Operations in Syria and Iraq" (16 September 2016), accessed online <www.publication.parliament.uk>.

United Kingdom, Cabinet Office, "PM statement to the House on Libya," 21 March 2011. accessed through <https://www.gov.uk/government/speeches/pm-statement-to-the-house-on-libya>.

United Kingdom, Cabinet Office, *UK action to combat Daesh*. Accessed through <https://www.gov.uk/government/topical-events/daesh/about>.

United Kingdom, House of Commons Defence Select Committee. "Written evidence from the Ministry of Defence: Government response" in "Afghanistan report 2013-14," accessed through <http://data.parliament.uk/writtenevidence/committeeevidence.svc/evidencedocument/defence-committee/afghanistan/written/6948.html>.

United Kingdom, Houses of Parliament debate, "UK Special Forces: Iraq and Afghanistan" in: *Hansard*. Vol 669. accessed through <https://hansard.parliament.uk/Commons/2020-01-07/debates/4B913D4B-8058-456B-A485-B56C447DE042/UKSpecialForcesIraqAndAfghanistan>.

United Kingdom, Houses of Parliament debate, "Yemen" in: *Hansard*, vol 689. Accessed through <https://hansard.parliament.uk/commons/2021-02-08/debates/DD75DAB2-90FB-42FF-B3EC-095A91F0C49B/Yemen>.

United Kingdom, Ministry of Defence, "Memorandum submitted by the Ministry of Defence for House of Commons Defence Select Committee Report: UK Military Operations in Syria and Iraq" (1 December 2015). accessed www.data.parliament.uk, last accessed 7 May 2021.

United Kingdom. "Hansard Houses of Commons Debate" 9 February 1944 Column 737. <https://api.parliament.uk/historic-hansard/lords/1944/feb/09/bombing-policy>.

United Kingdom. "House of Commons Defence Select Committee: Report UK Military Operations in Syria and Iraq," accessed through <https://publications.parliament.uk/pa/cm201617/cmselect/cmdfence/106/10602.htm>.

United Kingdom. "Prime Minister's response to the Foreign Affairs Select Committee' second report of session 2015-16: The Extension of Offensive British Military Operations to Syria." Foreign Affairs Select Committee. Memorandum to the Foreign Affairs Select Committee. November 2015.

United Kingdom. All Party Parliamentary Group Parliamentary Questions. Accessed through <http://appgdrones.org.uk/parliamentary-questions/>.

United Kingdom. Defence and Security Media Advisory (DSMA) Committee, "Notice on Military counter terrorist forces, Special Forces and Intelligence Agency Operations, Activities and Communications methods and techniques," last accessed 25 May 2021, through <https://dsma.uk/notice/military-counter-terrorist-forces-special-forces-and-intelligence-agency-operations-activities-and-communication-methods-and-techniques/>.

United Kingdom. Foreign and Commonwealth Office, "Minister Elwood statement on Mosul," 17 October 2016. Accessed through <https://www.gov.uk/government/news/minister-ellwood-statement-on-mosul>.

United Kingdom. *Hansard Houses of Commons Debate* (1 December 1943): Vol 395. <https://hansard.parliament.uk/Commons/1943-12-01/debates/81abbcb0-c2f3-4f48-87b5-7846e2d35e44/BombingPolicy>.

United Kingdom. *Hansard Houses of Commons Debate* (21 March 2011): Column 708 <www.hansard.parliament.uk>.

United Kingdom. *Hansard Houses of Commons Debate* (7 September 2015): *Column 25*, <www.hansard.parliament.uk>.

United Kingdom. *Hansard Houses of Commons Debate*. 12 December 1944: vol 406. Accessed through <https://api.parliament.uk/historic-hansard/commons/1944/dec/12/bombing-targets-germany>.

United Kingdom. HM Government Press release, "PM to announce largest military investment in 30 years (2020)", last accessed March 1, 2021 through <https /www.gov.uk/government/news/>.

United Kingdom. House of Commons Defence Select Committee. "Government response" in *Afghanistan report 2013-14*. Accessed through <https://publications.parliament.uk/pa/cm201415/cmselect/cmdfence/582/58204.htm>.

United Kingdom. House of Commons Defence Select Committee. "Written evidence from the Ministry of Defence: Oral evidence" for *Afghanistan report 2013-14*. Accessed through <https://publications.parliament.uk/pa/cm201012/cmselect/cmdfence/554/10102602.htm>.

United Kingdom. House of Commons Foreign Affairs Select Committee. "International Law" in "Kosovo Fourth report," May 3, 2000. Accessed through <https://publications.parliament.uk/pa/cm199900/cmselect/cmfaff/28/2814.htm>.

United Kingdom. Houses of Parliament debate. "Falkland Islands" in: *Hansard,* vol. 23, May 4, 1982. Accessed through <https://api.parliament.uk/historic-hansard/commons/1982/may/04/falkland-islands-2>.

United Kingdom. Houses of Parliament debate. "The Gulf" in *Hansard,* vol. 186. May 26, 1991. Accessed through <https://api.parliament.uk/historic-hansard/commons/1991/feb/26/the-gulf>.

United Kingdom. Ministry of Defence, "Annual Population Survey: UK Armed Forces Veterans residing in Great Britain, 2017" (31 January 2019), last accessed 7 May 2021 through <https://assets.publishing.service.gov.uk/government/uploads/system/uploads/attachment_data/file/774937/20190128_-_APS_2017_Statistical_Bulletin_-_OS.pdf>.

United Kingdom. Ministry of Defence, "Defence in the media: 24 October 2016," <https://modmedia.blog.gov.uk/2016/10/24/defence-in-the-media-24-october-2016/>.

United Kingdom. Ministry of Defence, "Defence Secretary welcomes Iraqi Victory in Mosul," 10 July 2017. Assessed through <www.gov.uk/goverment/news/defence-secretary-welcomes-iraqi-victory-in-mosul>.

United Kingdom. Ministry of Defence, *Global Britain in a competitive age: The integrated Review of Security, Defence, Development and Foreign Policy* (2021).

United Kingdom. Ministry of Defence. "Defence Secretary announces extension of UK training mission to Ukraine," November 4, 2019. Accessed through <https://www.gov.uk/government/news/defence-secretary-announces-extension-of-uk-training-mission-to-ukraine>.

United Kingdom. Ministry of Defence. "Defence Secretary announces extension of support to Ukraine's armed forces." September 21, 2018, <https://www.gov.uk/government/news/defence-secretary-announces-extension-of-support-to-ukraines-armed-forces>.

United Nations, United Nations Security Council Resolution 1973 (17 March 2011).

Van Creveld, M. "The Transformation of War Revisited," in: *Small Wars & Insurgencies* 13, no. 2 (2002): 3–15.

Van Creveld, M. *Transformation of War* (New York: Free Press, 1991).

Van der Meulen, J. "Bombing ISIS. Public Support and Public Dilemmas" in: Heeren-Bogers, J. *et al.* (eds.) *The Yin-Yang Military* (Springer, Cham. 2020).

Waal, J. de, YouGov., "British attitudes to drones" YouGov April 3, 2013 accessed through <https://yougov.co.uk/topics/politics/articles-reports/2013/04/03/british-attitudes-drones-and-targeted-killing>.

Waal, J. de "British Attitudes to drones" YouGov. April 3, 2013, accessed through <https://yougov.co.uk/topics/politics/articles-reports/2013/04/03/british-attitudes-drones-and-targeted-killing>.

Waal, J. de "Report of British Attitudes to Defence, Security and Armed Forces." YouGov. October 25, 2014. Accessed through <https://yougov.co.uk/topics/international/articles-reports/2014/10/25/report-british-attitudes-defence-security-and-arme>.

Walker, P. "De Menezes: what the police said in 2005," in: *The Guardian*. August 2, 2007. Accessed through <https://www.theguardian.com/uk/2007/aug/02/menezes.peterwalker1>.

Waltz, K., *Foreign Policy and Democratic Politics* (Longmans: London, 1968).

Warfare.Today. "RAF plays it Part in re-taking Mosul," 10 July 2017, accessed through <http://www.warfare.today/2017/07/10/raf-plays-its-part-in-re-taking-mosul/>.

Whetham, D. "Killer Drones: the moral ups and down," in *The RUSI Journal.* 158.3: 22–32.

Whetham, D. "Neither Victors nor Victims" in: Hom, A., O'Driscoll, C. and Mills, K. *Moral Victories: The Ethics of Winning Wars,* (2017): 176–198.

Whetham, David. "Killer Drones: The Moral Ups and Downs," in *The RUSI Journal* 158, no. 3 (2013): 22–32.

Whiteley, P. *et al.*, "Why Do Voters Lose Trust in Governments? Public Perceptions of Government Honesty and Trustworthiness in Britain 2000–2013," in: *British Journal of Politics & International Relations* 18, no. 1 (2016): 234–254.

Wintour, P. and Norton-Taylor, R. "No Challenges civilian death toll," in *The Guardian.* October 30, 2004. Accessed through <https://search.proquest.com/docview/246218899/4F98FD4760474366PQ/38?accountid=11862>.

YouGov. "A former SAS sergeant is being investigated for murder after admitting to "mercy killings" – killing mortally wounded enemy soldiers – in Iraq, who he claimed pleaded with him to do it. Do you think mercy killings like this are acceptable or unacceptable?" October 17, 2016. Accessed through <https://yougov.co.uk/topics/philosophy/survey-results/daily/2016/10/17/e7340/1>.

YouGov. "Do you think that the UK does or does not carry out similar attacks in other parts of the world?" May 13, 2018. Accessed through <https://yougov.co.uk/topics/travel/survey-results/daily/2018/03/13/d167e/2>.

YouGov. "Should it be necessary or not necessary for Parliament to vote on whether or not we take part in military action against Syria by the US and its allies?" April 12, 2018. Accessed through <https://yougov.co.uk/topics/politics/survey-results/daily/2018/04/12/5a002/1>.

YouGov. Poll, "Some Western governments have recently been linked with the policy of assassination or "targeted killing" of individuals deemed a threat to security. To what extent, if at all, would you support or oppose your country's government taking part or assisting in each of the following?" February 26-27, 2013. Accessed through <http://cdn.yougov.com/cumulus_uploads/document/7jhe13wtc6/YGCam-Archive-results-270213-Assassination-Drones.pdf>.

Yu, J. *Follow the golden rule.* Last accessed May 25, 2021 through <https://www.york.ac.uk/research/themes/golden-rule/>.